The *Working Mother* Book of TIME

St. Martin's Griffin

New York

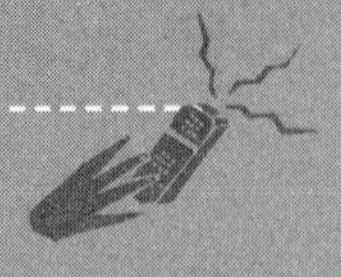

The *Working Mother* Book of TIME

How to

TAKE IT, MAKE IT, SAVE IT, *and* SAVOR IT

From the Editors of *Working Mother* Magazine

Grateful acknowledgment is given to the readers of *Working Mother* magazine whose comments are included in this book and used by permission.

Book design by Judith Stagnitto Abbate/Abbate Design

ISBN 0-312-26273-6

First Edition: May 2000

10 9 8 7 6 5 4 3 2 1

Contents

Acknowledgments

The creation of this book was a collaborative process, drawing on the insights of many people who so generously found time for this project.

First, I'd like to thank the editors of *Working Mother* magazine, past and present, for their contributions of talent and enthusiasm. In particular, we owe the writer of this book, Catherine Cartwright, a former senior editor at the magazine, a debt of gratitude. She labored diligently to create a useful and interesting volume, spending many evenings and weekends to bring together the collective wisdom of our readers and staff. On Catherine's behalf, I'd like to express her thanks (and ours) to her friend Jeff Holecko, and to Carol Cartwright, Catherine's very own working mother. Their love and encouragement, and that of all Catherine's family and friends, were a tremendous support.

Many thanks also to Jay MacDonald, Founder/Chairman, WorkingWomanNetwork, Inc., for his commitment to developing a line of

Working Mother books. We couldn't have produced this book without the help of others who shepherded and tweaked it from its initial stages through the final manuscript: Kalia Doner at D&M Publishing, Regula Noetzli, our agent, and Marian Lizzi at St. Martin's Press.

Most of all, I'd like to thank the more than 1,500 members of the *Working Mother* reader panel, a group of women who regularly share their experiences, opinions, and expertise with us. Hundreds of them took the time to complete an extensive survey about their own time-management habits, problems, and solutions. The book wouldn't be the same without their observations, which you'll find on nearly every page. All of us at *Working Mother* were deeply impressed by their participation and their interest not only in improving their own lives but in helping others.

LISA R. BENENSON
Editor in Chief
Working Mother

Introduction

You're already a veteran of the time wars. Every day, as a busy working mom, you must figure out how to squeeze in the often-overlapping demands of work, home, and kids. So what can this book offer you?

A new approach to what we call *time arrangement* and a mix of innovative solutions, sympathy, and support.

Working Mother has distilled the most useful time-arrangement strategies suggested and tested by moms like you. These are strategies that work for *real* life—ideas that will help you gain time, and *enjoy* the time you've gained. We can do this because no one knows working moms like *Working Mother.*

For more than twenty years, we've been serving the very special needs of busy women who balance work and family. Millions of subscribers have depended on us to give them helpful information in an easy-to-read, get-to-the-point format. Our readers have told us what they think, letting us know when we've struck a chord and when we've missed the boat. Mostly, they've thanked us for understanding them, helping them, and affirming them (one reader even called *Working Mother* magazine "a support group I can hold in my hands").

In putting together the best strategies from the files of *Working Mother* magazine, we have discovered, once again, just how resourceful, insightful, and determined working women are. Here is that wisdom, distilled for you.

| PART ONE |

TIME THIEVES

How to Avoid Robbing Yourself of Family, Work, and Personal Time

Time management: The phrase is at once intimidating and irritating, conjuring up images of superefficient automatons dispensing fussy and useless advice to the harassed and haggard. Who needs it? Not you.

That's why we've created a book that offers more than simplistic tips about how to do two things at once or find a faster way to make a peanut butter sandwich. Here you can adopt a *new attitude* toward time and discover new systems to help you act on that attitude. We call this new approach *time arrangement.*

Spend a few minutes exploring this book, and you'll discover interesting ways to change your pace and ease stress. Our goal is to help you enjoy what you can accomplish and cheerfully accept what you can't get done. Here's how we'll proceed.

In this first part, **Time Thieves,** there are chapters that will help you make friends with time and learn how to accept what you can—and can't—accomplish in a day. And you'll find out how to break the hold of the big three time thieves: mother's guilt, procrastination, and sweating the small stuff.

In Part Two, **Family Time,** you can explore ways to reduce the daily maintenance required to run a family—and to increase the fun times you share with your children and mate. Topics include:

- **organizing shortcuts:** the family calendar and the to-do lists
- **hour-by-hour revamp:** the trouble spots of your day, such as hectic mornings and drawn-out bedtimes, with suggested solutions
- **housework:** including how you can involve your husband and children
- **weekends:** handling errands and kids' activities while fitting in fun
- **special family occasions:** holidays, birthday parties, and travel

Part Three, **Work Time,** offers suggestions on how to make the most of your job in the least amount of time. We cover:

- **mental tactics:** beating procrastination, making decisions quickly and effectively, reducing stress, keeping standards reasonable, learning to plan and prioritize
- **tools of the trade:** calendars and planners; computers, voice mail, and other technologies; filing and storage solutions
- **acting:** delegating, working efficiently, using your lunch hour to the fullest, managing business travel, exploring and winning alternative work options
- **reacting:** recovering from mistakes, handling difficult coworkers, coping with interruptions, and handling overtime requests

The last section, Part Four, **Personal Time,** focuses on the Holy Grail. Whether you have a hard time putting yourself first—even for a few hours a week—or you want to have solo time but can't find it, the strategies in this section will help you claim these vital, rejuvenating hours. We examine new ways to define your relationships with:

- **your spouse**
- **your friends**
- **yourself alone**
- **exercise**
- **hobbies**
- **your community**

We hope these pages will inspire, inform, and guide you. You're already doing the toughest, most satisfying job out there—being a working mom. We aim to smooth your path and send you on your way with a smile.

| 1 |

Get Time on Your Side . . .

Or, How I Learned to Banish Guilt, Accept My Limitations, and Take Pride in My Accomplishments

Time has become the enemy. Not that it has ever done anything wrong; it moves along at the same constant tempo, sunrise to sunset, June to July, as it always has. But modern society has altered our sense of time. We have adopted destructive attitudes about both how it should be used (immediately, frantically) and how it passes (too quickly). As a result, we feel that we don't have enough time or enough control over the time we have. Recent research reveals five forces that contribute to our troubled relationship to time.

1. **Leisure time is fragmented.** Despite the fact that Americans have about five hours more leisure time each week than they did in 1965, and—get this—the average working mom has about thirty hours a week "free," most of those leisure hours come in hard-to-use bits and pieces: five or ten minutes of free time at the breakfast table, fifteen minutes between dinner and helping the kids with their homework, twenty minutes before bed. We

feel frustrated because these short stretches of downtime are so often frittered away. We haven't learned how to enjoy them.

2. **There is pressure to do everything as quickly as possible.** A common compulsion is what one expert calls "urgency addiction," the drive to go faster and faster, all day, every day. "People who suffer from this syndrome lose their inner sense of time and gradually live in a world where time is distorted," says Nina Tassi, the author of *Urgency Addiction: How to Slow Down Without Sacrificing Success.* Even when they aren't overloaded with work and responsibility, they feel harried. Time-use experts John Robinson, of the University of Maryland, and Geoffrey Godbey, of Penn State University, have monitored this growing sense of time pressure over the past three decades. In a 1965 study, they found that 24 percent of respondents *always* felt rushed. By the 1990s, that figure had risen to 38 percent.
3. **There are too many choices about how to spend our time.** We feel busier because of something Robinson calls "over-choice." "There are more clubs to join, more magazines and books to read, and more television stations to flip through," he says. "We end up filling up our time with things we don't necessarily want to do."
4. **Technology creates complications.** Advances in technology and telecommunications add to that rushed sensation by ratcheting up the possibilities. There's always a way to do more, to do it better, to do it faster. Why send out an annual holiday letter when you can make a family Web site instead?
5. **We don't feel confident about how we choose to spend our time.** Expectations are so high today—more than half of working women say they think they should be able to work full-time and cook at least five dinners a week—that it's easy to become critical about what you actually accomplish or the choices you are forced to make about how to spend your time. And that can lead to anxiety about how to allocate the time available or about being a good enough parent, employee, wife, or friend. As a result of these pressures, it's difficult for even the most organized and calm-thinking working mom to feel good about how she spends her minutes and hours. More than one third of mothers

surveyed in a *Working Mother* time-management study said that the way they use their time makes them feel inadequate and frustrated.

So how can you make use of those 30 "free" hours and increase your enjoyment of the remaining 138 hours in your week?

You can learn to arrange your time in new and more useful ways—first by changing your attitude toward time and then by backing up your new attitude with systems that keep life running smoothly.

The New Attitude: "It's good enough for me!"

Enough with second-guessing and guilty feelings! As a mom, you are the center of your children's universe. This is true. But that doesn't mean you are required to be perfect or to take on everything the world dumps at your feet. Still, some days (maybe *every* day) you feel you are. And since you are rarely perfect and often fallible, funny, friendly, ferocious, and frequently fretful, you may also be prone to second-guessing your every move, wondering if you did the right thing, made the right choice.

Before you know it you've set off an avalanche of regret and guilt—and all you did was decide to keep your four-year-old in child care an extra hour a day or agree to take on another project at work.

"I think mothers sometimes experience a kind of anticipatory guilt," says Lisa Silberstein, Ph.D., a psychologist and therapist in private practice in Connecticut. In a study Silberstein did of two-career couples, she found that many women predicted that they would feel tremendously guilty about using child care for their kids. "Instead, once they went back to work, they usually found that their babies were quite happy in day care and that they had no reason to feel guilty. It's helpful to realize that a lot of things we think we should feel guilty about don't necessarily get borne out in reality," says Silberstein.

Still, a vicious cycle of guilt persists for some mothers. "If I ever spend time on myself, I feel guilty about it. I feel I should be spending all my available time with my children to make up for all the time I am not spending on them when I am working," says Lynn Rosario, a New

Jersey account executive and mother of a two-year-old and a five-year-old. The end result: No time is well spent. Other moms echo Rosario's discontent: "If I'm at work, I feel guilty that I'm not at home; if I'm at home, I feel guilty that I'm not at work," says one. Dr. Silberstein's reaction: "Gaps between what we think is the ideal and what turns out to be real are what cause guilt. Sometimes, guilt is useful because it alerts you to an imbalance, an area where you need to make a change. But when it is impossible to make a change, living in a state of constant friction is devastating."

It's tough to let go of guilt, says Silberstein, because it means committing to a choice and living with it. "Guilt is a way to play out both sides. It keeps you a half step away from taking a very different path. If a woman is locked into guilt that she's not doing this for her kids and that for her house, she may not ask her husband to contribute or decide to hire a housecleaner, for example—maybe because in her experience, 'good mothers don't need help.' "

Although it may seem hard to let go of these time-wasting, anxious feelings, you can if you set your mind to it. Follow the lead of accomplished working mom Kristine Malkoski. "I made a conscious choice to stop second-guessing my decisions and not to feel guilty or bad about them. I trained myself to do what I thought was best, then let go and move on," says Malkoski, the mother of three small children and the president and chief operating officer of the Pharmaceutical Corporation of America. "That's not to say that I never again stopped to examine an experience and see if I might learn something from it. Rather, it was a new strategy to put an end to unnecessary guilt and worry," Malkoski continues. "This attitude has given me a lot of confidence and helped me to move ahead in the business world. Without the burden of second-guessing, I also enjoy life more and feel I have accomplished more than when I was wasting time constantly reviewing my decisions."

Four Steps to Banishing Guilt

1. **Stop trying to be perfect.** Unreasonable personal expectations are one of the most common guilt-provokers for women. Too

many women expect to excel in all areas. It's fine to be competent in many, many different areas, but if your standards are too high and are making you unhappy, it's time for a reality check.

One working mother told me the story of her kitchen makeover. "It was fabulous," she reports. "But one thing they talked me into was painting my beaten-up wood floor white. I soon found myself every weekend on my hands and knees cleaning those floors," she says. It made her feel stressed when she did it and guilty when she didn't. "Was I happy? No. Was my family happy? Absolutely not," she says. "I became a tyrant, resentful of every spill. I felt all my work was unappreciated. My family couldn't have cared less."

Then one day she asked herself why she was doing this. She realized she was remembering her grandmother, a meticulous housewife. "As a child, I heard over and over again, 'Her house is so clean you can eat off the floors.' So there I was, abusing my family, spoiling my weekends, because of my grandmother's values." Those values of immaculate cleanliness were fine for Grandmother. Her job was homemaker. But if you're working full-time *and* being a homemaker, you don't need or want perfect floors. "That weekend we laid down a wonderful, durable tile floor that hides the little spills. It was amazing how that changed my stress level instantly."

This is how negative guilt is born. People from the past, or people from the present whom we may not even like, make us set unrealistic standards. So whenever you have an attack of unwarranted guilt, ask yourself if your standards are realistic and really your own. Compete with yourself, not others.

2. **Set your true goals.** This takes a lot of soul-searching and thought. Is one of your life goals to have a pristine home, or is your goal to have a home that feels comfortable, loving, pressure free? Is your goal to be available to your children twenty-four hours a day, or to be refreshed, loving, and sensitive when you are with them?

   Put your goals on paper and post them on the refrigerator so you can refer to them often. You need to internalize them, because there are going to be dozens of times a day when you have to make choices. Those choices will be easier, less guilt-inducing, if you make them with your goals in mind.

3. **Be a timely time manager.** To manage guilt successfully, you have to be mindful of the moment, to be ready to act *now.* Let's say you've set as your goal to be an attentive, loving mother. Here's the situation: You're picking your child up from school. You're in a rush because you need to stop by the store, make dinner, clean up, run a load of laundry, supervise homework, and so on. You get to school and your child looks grumpy. You're at a crossroads. It's time for a choice. Review your goals. Sooner or later, the anger or frustration you saw on that face is going to be expressed.

   "Hey, I've got an idea," you might say. "Let's stop at the playground and swing for a few minutes before we go to the store. I want to talk with you and find out about your day." Five minutes of attention and mindfulness, as psychologists call it, can save an hour of tension and tears later on.

   Similarly, you may set a goal of fitting fitness into your life. On a day you find yourself unexpectedly able to leave work early, you have several options: stay at work anyway to catch up, exercise, run errands, or pick up your kids from child care early. If your goal is to work out more—since you know that it benefits you and your family—you'll choose that option, with much less guilt. That's timely guilt-management. Remember, you're never *not* busy.

4. **Get organized.** When your life is well managed, you're not always operating from a crisis mode and things don't slip through the cracks to make you feel guilty.

| 2 |

Put Off Procrastination

How to Take Care of the Most Important Tasks Today, So They Don't Haunt Your Tomorrows

It's funny how NOT doing something can waste time, but that's the real disadvantage of procrastination. When you put off attending to important tasks, not only do you spend time thinking about what you are not doing, a task delayed almost always becomes a larger production to accomplish when you do finally get around to it.

"Procrastination, more than anything else I can think of, separates those who want to be successful from those who are," says Lee Silber, author of *Time Management for the Creative Person.* "It's the difference between being a dreamer and a doer, someone who says to the world, 'This is what I'm going to do,' then backs it up with action."

For working moms, the list of things that can be put off is enormous and confusing—more time with your kids, more time at work, less time at work, more time exercising, less time commuting, talking to your child-care provider about problems at preschool, talking to teachers, mowing the lawn, getting your hair cut. You name it, it's a candidate for the great to-do sometime list in the sky.

Where to Begin?

Your first step in overcoming procrastination is to tease out the psychological hurdle that's preventing you from beginning a project or making a tough decision. Is it fear of failure? Does the task you need to do intimidate you? Are you delaying because you must do something you don't enjoy or something you resent having to do? Then you can work to resolve the underlying cause (apprehension, anxiety, lack of skills or support) instead of its symptom—procrastination.

Why Do You Procrastinate?

Lee Silber identifies these as some of the most common reasons people procrastinate. Which ones sound familiar to you?

- Perfectionism: If you can't do it right, you won't do it at all (see "Don't Sweat the Small Stuff," page 13).
- You need the adrenaline rush of waiting until the last minute to get going.
- There is no immediate payoff for doing it now, so you postpone it while you do something that *does* have an immediate payoff.
- You hope it will just go away (or that someone else will do it for you).
- You don't want to do it.
- You don't know how to do it.
- It's boring.
- You're afraid of failing.
- Your environment makes it impossible to take this on right now (no room to work, noise, distractions).
- You're easily sidetracked (see "Coping with Inter . . . rup . . . tions," page 116).
- You're waiting for inspiration to hit.
- You're not in the mood.
- You don't know where to begin.

- There's no deadline or the deadline is distant, so you don't need to start yet.
- You're overcommitted.
- You can live with the results of not doing it.

Moving Beyond Procrastination

All-purpose procrastination stoppers:

- If the task you need to do is too large and overwhelming, break it down into more manageable pieces. Don't set out to clean the entire attic or plan every detail of a two-week vacation. Instead, resolve to clear just one section of the attic, or do just one task a day related to the vacation (schedule flights, reserve a hotel room, surf the Internet for activity ideas).
- "Worst first": Get distasteful jobs out of the way early whenever possible. "This gives you the burst of energy you need to finish," says Silber.
- Make a written commitment of your goal or a list of intermediate steps. Include a deadline. Then schedule ironclad appointments—write them down, too—for the times when you'll work on the project.
- Find an easier way around a dreaded task. Hate talking on the phone? Dash off an E-mail. Or delegate the job you've been avoiding to a spouse, child, or paid pro.
- Do absolutely nothing for a few minutes—literally, don't move a muscle. You'll be dying to work after that.
- Make visual reminders that can't be ignored: Tape a bright orange note to your computer monitor, refrigerator, mirror, or telephone. Use this tactic for words of inspiration, too!
- Get help. Find someone to share the task with. Or recruit a buddy to encourage you as you work: Ask a coworker, a friend, or your mate to check in with you periodically and deliver a few friendly words of encouragement.
- Grant yourself a small reward after you've completed part of the task, and a big one after you've done the whole thing!

| 3 |

Don't Sweat the Small Stuff

A Slightly Zen Guide to Letting Go of Perfectionism and Learning to Let Unimportant Stuff Slide Right on By

Another major time thief is perfectionism, a common stumbling block for working mothers who are so often determined to be the best at the many roles they must fill. For some, it shows up only around the house, for others only at work, and for the truly burdened, it hounds them whatever they do. Well, *Working Mother* is here to tell you that this is one of the least productive impulses you can have—at least according to the hundreds of moms across the country who have let us know how hard they fight to overcome the compulsion. Sure, it's important to do your homework conscientiously and completely. Once in a while, it's great to dazzle your family by going above and beyond the call of duty. But an obsessive need to reach an impossible standard is counterproductive. You'll never be finished with what you're doing, or satisfied with it if you're forced to stop, because there's no way it can ever be perfect. And for some women, the fear of being less than perfect becomes immobilizing; they are unable to begin projects because they worry that they won't do them "right."

If any of this sounds familiar, you're in a great position to recapture hours a week of potentially enjoyable time: Just throw out the desire to be perfect and substitute the desire to be less stressed and get more done! To set that just-right standard:

- Learn, by observing and talking with others, how to tell when something is good enough, and then how to let it go.
- Consider: What are the consequences of your perfectionism on your work and your personal life? For example, are you constantly late for the evening child-care pickup because you need to do "just one more thing" or redo the memo you've been writing one last time?
- Ask yourself: Is this worth the effort I'm expending on it? Will anyone notice, care, or appreciate the final result?
- Stop yourself when you stew over a mistake. Learn from it and move on (see page 113).
- In situations where you know you're likely to let perfectionism get the best of you, give yourself a time limit. Say, "I'll revise this document/sew this costume/clean this kitchen for the next half an hour. After that, I'll move on to something else."

| PART TWO |

FAMILY TIME

How to Enjoy the Time You Have with Your Family—and How to Find More Time Together

The daily effort required to run a family is staggering and seems to expand exponentially when both parents work outside the home. There is food to prepare, clothing to wash, bills to pay. But most important, there are special people to care for, enjoy, and love. How can we spend enough time with them—and still keep up with all the chores we must do in order to stay afloat? In this section we'll outline the strategies and shortcuts you can employ to minimize work—and maximize fun.

Underlying it all is a new definition of "family time." Think about it: What does family time mean to you? Is it a holiday table groaning with food and surrounded by relatives? A day spent working side by side in the backyard garden? A beach vacation? Or simply a quiet walk to school?

We think all of these moments are family time. We can enjoy our children and spouses every day—not just on special occasions. Opportunities for connection abound in brief, commonplace moments: A fifteen-minute walk to school with your second-grader is a chance for hearty conversation or silly songs. Folding a fluffy load of warm laundry can be a joint project—for husband and wife, brother and sister, or parent and child. A short bedtime routine of bath, snack, and story can become a beloved family ritual.

In this section we examine all these issues:

- **Figuring Out Family Time** (Chapter 4) offers organizational strategies and attitude adjustments to help you use the time you have more satisfactorily and to increase the time you can spend together.
- **A Day in the Life** (Chapter 5) takes you through the day from your 6 A.M. wake-up to lights-out; it offers practical advice for managing every step in your family's day.
- **Getting a Handle on Housework** (Chapter 6) presents techniques

for getting your whole family (particularly your husband) to pitch in and suggestions for how to step back and let things go—plus tips on shopping and laundry.

- **Weekends** (Chapter 7) looks at the great weekend debate—fun or family work?—and shows you how to get both done and still have some time for yourself.
- **Special Family Occasions** (Chapter 8) wraps up the family section by looking at great ways to handle travel, birthdays, and holidays—three potentially high-stress times for the whole family.

4

Figuring Out Family Time

Do you long to spend more time with your children and partner? You're not alone. One survey we conducted revealed that close to 50 percent of moms wish they had more hours in the day to devote to family bonding (the rest of the moms said they need time for themselves—and sleep!). But don't throw up your hands in despair. You can overcome these frustrations without adding hours to the day—or giving up sleep. To give your family a time makeover all you need to do is:

- Redefine family time
- Just Say No
- Reorganize!

Redefining Family Time

We're so brainwashed about quality time that we often completely discount the importance of ordinary moments spent together during the course of a day—time getting ready in the morning, sharing the ride to school, grocery shopping or doing laundry, getting dinner on the table, walking the dog.

Children respond positively to being integrated into the texture of the day. They may love it if you block off a whole day for a trip to the zoo or spend an entire afternoon together, but what truly cements family connection and warmth is everyday involvement. And you've got plenty of that, if you will just take notice. So stop beating yourself up because you can't spend fantasy-perfect hours playing with your family at some idyllic getaway. Take pleasure and pride in the ordinary interactions that define your relationships and you will set a warm and comforting tone for the whole house.

One extra advantage to this new approach to family time: It encourages you to cherish your children, your partner, and the life you're building together every day. As Jacquelyn Mitchard, mother of five and the author of *The Deep End of the Ocean,* wrote: "My mother gave me the sense to appreciate light traffic, spaghetti for dinner, a good book waiting upstairs. There always would be a jewel in the ordinary clay of work or school. In the Bible it says that each day's evil is sufficient to that day. What my mother believed, without being an overbearing Pollyanna about it, is that so is each day's joy. There might be only a little. The look of the sky before a storm. Getting all the laundry done. But something.

"She sensed—and taught me—that the aggregate of all the little things is, finally, all we have. Big things don't turn up often enough to spend time pining after them. Ordinary life is the big thing. She had the knack of appreciating it."

Don't Get Stuck in a Rut

Families are always growing and changing. Time arrangements that work one year may not be practical the next. For example, when kids are young it may be possible to eat dinner together each evening, but it often becomes a struggle in school years when kids are busy with sports practices, lessons, and Scouts. When that happens, change the way you plan to spend time together. Perhaps breakfast will become your important family meal, or you can aim to convene the family for a 9 P.M. snack.

Just Say No

You can't find more—or more pleasing—time with your family if you say yes to every relative, colleague, and neighbor who asks you to do something. You have to know what matters to you and then eliminate anything that keeps you from fulfilling your priorities. That means you need an underlying set of goals. Is one of your goals to help your children maximize their creative potential? Then you'll trade overtime opportunities at work for music-lesson carpools. Or perhaps your aim is to restore an old home and turn it into a cozy family retreat. Then you might decide to pass on a leadership role in the PTA or the Boy Scouts so your weekends will be free for renovation work.

The point is, you'll need to make decisions based on how the options you're weighing help you meet your goals. Sometimes this may mean giving up a favorite hobby or cutting back on socializing with friends because work and family are more important to you right now. Or you may realize that something you don't enjoy doing—such as housecleaning or commuting—can be delegated, reduced, or eliminated. It may take you a while to get the hang of it; saying no isn't easy for most people. Only 35 percent of moms surveyed in *Working Mother*'s time study reported that they use "No" as a time-management technique; but more than half of all respondents say it is *the* time-saving technique they need to improve or do more of.

"I am learning to say no by thinking about whether whatever request I'm considering accomplishes my goal of spending more time with my children," says Linda Bookey of Washington State, a single mom to two boys and a self-employed business consultant. Bookey has the right idea. She knows to use the word *no* early and often, and to remember the big picture.

That's why mother of three Michele D. Marrie put her foot down when her two daughters' dance lessons interfered too much with family time. "When the lessons required six nights per week, including four sessions each Saturday, I finally woke up," says Marrie, a financial manager from Maryland. "My golden rule on this is, activities are to be a part of life, not life itself. If an activity becomes the driving force of most of your time, it has failed this test."

Reorganize!

If you wonder what other moms have to say about their priorities, the *Working Mother* time-management study found that 71 percent felt that spending time with their spouse is very important and 96 percent said

WORKING MOM'S WORDS OF WISDOM

"Keep It Simple"

Of all the time-management lessons I've learned, KISS (Keep It Simple, Stupid) has been the one that has taken me the longest to integrate into my life. I've never been a perfectionist, but I do have certain expectations that I try to live up to: reasonable household cleanliness, nutritious meals, varied social activities for my children, etc. I rarely give my kids fast food for dinner, but I no longer hesitate to substitute a sandwich and veggie sticks for a hot cooked meal. As my children grow, I've learned that letting them play by themselves is often far more satisfying than filling up their days with scheduled activities. When I purchase new clothes, I refuse to buy those that require ironing. Furniture purchases have been made with time management in mind—I look for low-maintenance, dirt-resistant pieces that require minimal care. Even our social plans reflect our keep-it-simple philosophy, favoring casual dress, simple recipes, and a willingness to accept contributions of dessert or appetizers from our guests.

—**Nancy Collamer,** *married, career consultant, and mother of two girls, ages seven and ten* time with their children is very important. Of course, even after you've got your priorities in order, you and your family will still have plenty on your plate (if not, wouldn't life be boring?). So, you'll need to find a set of organizational strategies that work for all of you—and stick with them.

Strategy One: The Family Calendar

A prominently placed calendar, with roomy boxes for each day, is a must for every busy family. Mark everything here, from after-school lessons to out-of-the-ordinary work commitments to family outings. Some families use different-colored markers for each member of the family. You can also use initials or other shorthand, especially for recurring events.

Train family members to check and update the calendar faithfully. Grade schoolers (about age seven and up) can be expected to write in

Sunday	Monday	Tuesday	Wednesday	Thursday	Friday	Saturday
		1 Zach: t-ball 4–5:30	2 Alice: Hosp. board mtg 7–9	3 Zach: t-ball 4–5:30	4	5 Zach: t-ball game/Wilson Park 10:00 Liza: playdate w/ Sam 2–4
6	7	8 Zach: t-ball 4–5:30	9	10 Zach: t-ball 4–5:30	11 Alice: dentist 7:45 A.M. HALF-DAY OF SCHOOL *sign up for after-care	12 Zach: t-ball game/Thayer Park 11:00 Orch. concert 8:00 (7:15 pick up babysitter)
13	14 Marty away Ph. 351-220-7000 x 255	15 Zach: t-ball 4–5:30	16 Marty back	17 Zach: t-ball 4–5:30	18	19 Zach: t-ball game/Wilson Park 10:00
20 lunch at Gram's	21	22 Zach: t-ball 4–5:30	23 Conf. w/ Liza's teacher 5:15	24 Zach: t-ball 4–5:30	25	26 Zach: t-ball game/Thayer Park 11:00
27	28 NO SCHOOL	29 Zach: t-ball 4–5:30	30	31 Zach: t-ball 4–5:30		

their events on the calendar—if they don't, you won't guarantee that they'll have the transportation (not to mention the clean band uniform or wrapped party gift) they need.

If you're married or living with a partner, be sure to review the calendar together so you can share duties and prevent misunderstandings. Kids can also be included in this review session: Three- and four-year-olds can be involved in updates about upcoming events, and children age five and up will be able to contribute to the discussion and provide input.

Many families set aside time on Sundays to check their signals for the coming week. Says Marie Trenga, an army physician from Georgia and the mother of kids ages three, five, and seven: "My husband and I use this time to confirm plans for anything out of the routine. For example, if I'm giving a speech on Tuesday morning, I ask Brian to plan to drive the kids to day care that day."

Strategy Two: The To-Do List

"If it's not written down, I don't know about it!" says one *Working Mother* reader, and she's right. Keeping a list of tasks to complete is the best way to remember them, motivate yourself to do them, and appreciate your hard work when you're done. You may need one for yourself and another for family projects. One method doesn't fit all, but three good rules of thumb are:

- Keep the list in one consistent place, whether it's in your daily planner or calendar, on your computer at work, or posted in your kitchen.
- Set aside a regular time each day (or each hour!) to check it.
- Don't forget to savor the sense of accomplishment you get from crossing out something (and don't be ashamed to write it down and cross it out after the fact).

Family-management expert and author Kathy Peel recommends asking yourself, as you look at your list: "What should I **do**? What should I **delegate**? What can I **delete**?" This could winnow down your list considerably.

Peel also recommends dividing your list up into categories such as Food, Finances, Special Projects, and so on. California account executive Cheryl Layne Farrell employs a variation of this strategy. "I sort my personal to-do list into three columns: things away from the office (dry cleaner, dentist, exercise); things at home in the evening (reconcile checkbook, attend kids' events, complete forms for health-care expense account); and calls to make (stockbroker, doctor, ill church member)," explains Farrell, whose two children are one and seven years old.

"I cross things out on the list during the day to get a sense of achievement," says Farrell. "I put easy and hard stuff on the lists and try to make sure as many hard things get crossed off as easy things. I allow myself to feel okay if only one thing is crossed off, especially if it was a really big deal," Farrell continues. "I drop things off the list if they are carried over a few days. If they resurface, then I need to break the task down in parts so that I become more motivated to do it."

WORKING MOM'S WORDS OF WISDOM

"Use Your Imagination to Get Organized"

My most important time-management technique is visualization. As I am driving home in my car, I picture myself doing everything I plan to do that evening. Often I am able to improve my efficiency by seeing trouble spots. If I had planned to do the laundry after the kids go to bed, I picture myself tired and waiting for the dryer to stop. So I rearrange my image to see me throwing the clothes in the washer before I start supper, then in the dryer before we sit down to eat and then folding them after baths. I also use this technique to organize my workday while driving to work in the morning, or picture the week ahead to efficiently organize my errands. Not only does it allow me to be more efficient, but I arrive home much more refreshed than when I used to listen to the news or music. When I mentally plan, the whole day seems to run more smoothly.

—**Marie Trenga,** *married, army physician, and mother of three children, ages three, five, and seven*

Marie Trenga uses a similar grouping technique. "I have a whiteboard in the kitchen where I group ongoing projects or things I want to do by category (e.g., Finance—review insurance; Family—zoo trip; Yard—install driveway lights). It gives us a sense of accomplishment to wipe off complete tasks," says Trenga. A variation on the to-do list is a day-to-day reminder file, a version of what in the workplace is often called the "tickler file." Keep an accordion file with a pocket for each day of the month. Then store things according to when you need to do them. Mom of two, Mindi Brenner, a personal fitness trainer from Nevada, says that for her this strategy reduces stress: "Instead of worrying about it, I file it and deal with it when I need to. On those days that I have extra time, I look ahead in the file to see what I can get a head start on. It really works!"

5

A Day in the Life

Much working-mom stress is caused by the same troublesome episodes, repeated over and over. These moments may be minor when taken alone, but together they create a cumulative sense of tension and time pressure. Maybe you consistently rush out of the house in the morning, running late, and then always have to double back for something you've forgotten. Perhaps the dinner hour is a flash point for your family, often marked by kids' squabbles. Or maybe you're always behind on housework, which means you're often stuck without clean clothes or dishes.

These are the times of day to identify, reconsider, and reorganize. If you can smooth out these recurring trouble spots, you'll go a long way toward a calmer, happier, more relaxed day. Here's an hour-by-hour guide to a better day:

10 P.M.

Starting the Day Right . . . the Night Before

ASK ANY WORKING mom and she'll tell you the secret to a smooth, sane morning is what you do the night before. Plan and lay out everything you can: clothes for everyone, down to the last stocking, hair bow, and sneaker; breakfast dishes; permission slips, gym clothes, and musical instruments; lunches. Leave as little as possible to chance—you'll be thankful.

"No matter how tired I am, my books and the kids' are all in their bags and on the end table by the door before I go to bed, and shoes are set out where they can be found easily," says Jean Burris, a Kentucky college student and single mom of three. "How awful to think that the one thing my mother spent years trying to teach me was actually the key to sanity in the mornings!"

6:00 A.M.

Help Yourself First

YOUR BEST BET may be to wake up while everyone else is still slumbering. "I like to get up earlier than the rest of the family so I can get things done before anyone else is awake," says Lori Hultin of California, who has two daughters and is a public relations and marketing consultant.

Mother of two Lisa McElaney also finds that rising early starts her day off on the right foot. "I do best if I get enough sleep, wake early, and on alternate days sit and read the newspaper alone or exercise for forty-five minutes," says McElaney, an educational filmmaker from Massachusetts.

Exercise energizes. Here's how it works for California mom Kelly Johnson: "I work out at the gym before work in the morning. I put my good clothes in the car the night before. When I get up, I throw on the workout clothes (laid out the night before), brush my teeth, no makeup, and off I go in less than ten minutes," says Johnson, a support services manager and mom to a toddler and a first-grader.

Simplify Your Beauty Routine

You'll gain precious time.

- Get a low- (or no-) fuss haircut. Stylists often recommend time-pressed women wear their hair either very short or long. Short hair dries quickly and needs little styling; you can always put long locks in a ponytail or updo when you are in a rush.
- Invest in a consultation with a skilled stylist, who can advise you on a cut that's flattering as well as easy to care for. She'll show you how to work with—not against—your hair's natural tendencies. Once you've got a basic style in place, you can get maintenance trims at a lower-cost salon.
- If makeup is important to you, employ a similar strategy: Find your best look, whether through experimentation or a department-store makeover, and stick with it. Keep steps to a minimum by using shortcut products such as tinted moisturizers and blush/lipstick combos.
- Throw away products you no longer use (the shampoo that stings your eyes, the lipsticks you never remember to wear) so they don't clutter up your bathroom.
- Choose long-wearing makeup, like smudge-proof, stay-put lipsticks and foundations and waterproof mascara, to minimize the need for touch-ups.
- Save time in the morning by doing parts of your normal beauty regimen in the evening (showering, shaving, plucking eyebrows, giving yourself a manicure, etc.).
- Buy two of each of your favorite cosmetics and keep one set stashed at work, in case you don't have time at home to put it on.

Prevent Wardrobe Snafus

Many a morning delay can be blamed on clothing. Save yourself some last-minute changes by making sure everything in your closet is ready to go.

- Get rid of clothes that never feel right, don't match with anything else, or grow uncomfortable as the day wears on.
- Get rid of clothes you haven't worn in over a year. It's tempting to hang on to them, thinking you might someday wear them again, but chances are you won't. (Most people wear 80 percent of their clothes only 20 percent of the time, says New York City professional organizer Gloria Schaaf.) With less clutter in your closet, you'll have a better sense of what's in there—and you won't have to hunt for things. Another benefit: If your clothes aren't crammed together and have more room to actually hang, you likely won't have to spend as much time ironing.
- If you do need to iron, do it the night before. Not only will this save time in the morning, but you'll also be less tempted to waste time overthinking what you're going to wear and changing your mind. You can also hang less wrinkled items in the bathroom while you shower to steam them.
- Set aside items that need cleaning or mending; don't put them back into your closet or drawers until they're ready to wear.
- That goes double for hosiery—don't hang on to stockings with runs! You'll only drive yourself crazy trying to remember which ones can only go with long skirts or pants.
- Organize your closet by category: work clothes in one section, weekend clothes in another, dressy clothes in a third section, suggests household organizing expert Kathy Peel. Within each category, group like items together (skirts, pants, blouses).
- Try the color-scheme system—always buy white, navy, and gray, for example, so that most pieces in your wardrobe can go together and you don't need as many shoes, bags, and other accessories.
- Consider creating and posting a list of possible outfits, including accessories, inside your closet, says Peel.
- Use accessories such as scarves, handbags, and jewelry to update your look. They take up less closet space (and save money). A well-chosen accessory is also more versatile than a trendy blouse or skirt; you can use it to liven up lots of different outfits.

7:00 A.M.

Rise and Shine: Getting the Kids Up

GETTING YOURSELF UP and dressed is the easy part. Adding the kids into the mix is more challenging. Rousing them, dressing them, feeding them, and shepherding them out the door—each step can derail you. Here's what to keep in mind so that you can all walk out the door smiling.

As you wake children, especially preschoolers, be aware of biorhythms—the body's internal schedule. Some kids are naturally alert in the morning; others start very slowly and pick up speed. To figure out your child's pattern, be alert to recurring scenes. Do you battle over bedtime, meals, or naps? Early birds awaken easily but need a fairly strict routine for the rest of the day. Late risers can be tough to get out the door but are often more flexible and able to go with the flow the rest of the day. If you've got a slow riser, ease her into the day. Start by playing some soft music, then switch on the lights. Physical activity is a good way to get your slugabed going, as is a high-carbohydrate, high-protein breakfast such as oatmeal, eggs, or even a tuna fish sandwich, for energy.

Always allow yourself extra time so you'll be cushioned in the event of an emergency or just a small snag. Even ten or fifteen minutes can be very valuable. You'll all feel better if you don't have to rush. "My six-year-old daughter and I get up with plenty of time to spare. I like and insist that we start our days as pleasantly as possible, with enough time to see what mood she's in and to help her adjust if things just haven't started out right," says Mary Furrie of Texas, a single mom who works in financial services. When dressing little ones, simplicity counts. Slip babies and toddlers into their clothes while they're sleeping, or send them to child care in whatever they slept in. They'll surely need a change of clothes before the day is out, anyway.

For preschoolers, mix-and-match clothes are a lifesaver—and so is giving them some autonomy. Let them pick their own outfits (the night before, of course!) even if they come up with some gaudy combinations. As long as the clothes are weather appropriate and durable enough for school or child care, they're okay. Don't worry—your child's teachers have seen plenty of kids arrive in mismatched plaids and tutus with jeans. You can always send along another outfit in case your child rethinks her choice.

Don't stand for morning battles over kids' outfits. "We have a rule: The clothes must be picked out the night before, or the kids agree to wear whatever I choose," says New Jersey mother of two Connie Pizarro, a bank vice president.

7:45 A.M.

Time for Breakfast

IT'S IMPORTANT THAT everyone in the family eat breakfast. But it may not be that you all sit down together or eat the same thing. Many schools and child-care programs offer a morning meal to kids who arrive early, which can both save time at home and provide a nice transition for kids.

A busy weekday morning is usually not the time for a complicated, multicourse meal. On weekends, keep dishes simple and concentrate on sharing the meal together, if that's important to you and feasible. One mom, Lorri Cardwell-Casey of Arkansas, sweetens the meal by reading aloud to her kids as they eat. In another young family, mornings are a father-son affair: "My husband gets up with our fifteen-month-old baby at six A.M., changes him, and gives him a bottle," says Virginia Reese Coles, a Los Angeles–based sales manager. "Then they walk to Starbucks for coffee. They get back around seven A.M. and then I get up.

WORKING MOM'S WORDS OF WISDOM

"It's Alarming"

All children need their own alarm clocks; ones they pick out themselves, that they can set each night and turn off in the morning.

—**Lisa McElaney,** *educational filmmaker and mother of a six- and a twelve-year-old*

This gives me the extra hour of sleep that I need and it provides bonding time between my husband and my son."

Kids can also participate in breakfast prep from an early age. "I buy the small boxes of cereal and keep them in a cabinet the kids can reach," says Janet Chamberlain, whose sons are four and eight. "I put bowls out the night before. They can get their own cereal, and the oldest can pour milk and juice. If the juice is too big for him to handle, I pour sippers the night before," explains Chamberlain, a software engineer from New Hampshire.

Quick Breakfast Picks

Kids need to get about one third of their daily nutrient needs at breakfast, according to the American Dietetic Association (ADA). Study after study shows that for children and adults, breakfast truly is the most important meal of the day. For kids, this means having a meal with roughly two to three servings of grains (carbohydrates), one of protein, one of dairy, and one of fruit. Keep in mind that kid-sized stomachs call for kid-sized portions. Generally, one tablespoon of food per year of age is equal to one serving for kids. Easy-to-prepare choices include:

- cold cereal (keep on a low shelf so kids can serve themselves)
- instant oatmeal
- frozen waffles, pancakes, or French toast (buy, or freeze weekend leftovers)
- breakfast bars
- fruit
- yogurt
- cheese (even cold pizza counts, says the ADA!)
- graham crackers
- peanut butter and jelly sandwiches (topping anything with peanut butter is a quick way to add protein, but it should not be served to children younger than six or seven because of allergy risks)

- smoothie shakes (blend 1 cup each of milk, yogurt, and blueberries with 1 banana; add several ice cubes, if desired)
- popsicle made from smoothie mixture

8:00 A.M.

A Simple Routine Is Your Best Friend

DESPITE YOUR BEST efforts, someone in your family (your children, your spouse, you) will need prodding in the morning. Keep clocks in the bathrooms and kitchen—rooms where you spend a lot of prep time in the morning—to remind everyone to stay on track. Some kids respond well to reminders by kitchen timer. This turns the timer into the bad guy and spares you from being the nagger.

By far the best motivator and stress saver for little ones is a familiar routine. Lori Hultin shares her five-year-old daughter Shannyn's pattern: "On school mornings, she gets dressed, then eats breakfast, brushes her teeth and hair, and then if there is any time left over, she can pick a quiet activity until we are ready to leave. There is no TV watching on school mornings, as I find this makes her more lethargic and less likely to want to get up and move!" One way to help kids remember the plan is to post a list of things to do; use pictures for nonreaders. *Working Mother* readers have other great stick-to-it ideas:

- "One day I was having a particularly rough time getting my kids to get moving. I sat down with them and asked them if they realized what happens to me if I am late to work. I told them that I have to sit in time-out if I am late to work. This was a magical answer because it was something that they could identify with. They knew that they didn't want their mommy to have to do this. Sometimes, if one is dragging in the morning, they remind each other of this perilous doom that awaits me." —*Melinda Laughon,* sales manager and mother of two young kids, ages three and five, Roanoke, Virginia
- "My daughter loves for me to time her. If we're having trouble getting her going, we'll pretend she is in a race against the clock

and see how fast she can get dressed and brush her teeth and hair." —*Lori Hultin*

- "We have had to resort to a series of deadlines to keep the kids on schedule. During the school year, their alarms go off at 6 A.M. They have to be down to breakfast, clothes on and beds made, by 6:10. Breakfast must be done by 6:40. By 6:50 they are supposed to have their teeth brushed and shoes on. At 6:55 they each take their medication and get their jackets on and get in the car so we can drop them off at school at 7:00 on the way to work. For a while we had them earning coupons for computer play for making the various deadlines. We are now working with penalties: You miss more than two deadlines and you don't get to play Nintendo." —*Diane Ginther,* human resources manager and mom to two school-age boys, Shawnee, Kansas
- "To make sure my sons want to get in the car, I keep some of their favorite toys in the car, and they get to bring a sipper to drink. In the winter the sipper is hot cocoa, which they don't get to hold until they head for the car." —*Janet Chamberlain*

8:15 A.M.

Flexibility Rules

DESPITE YOUR BEST-LAID plans, you're bound to get socked with an unexpected obstacle from time to time: Your baby runs a fever, your car breaks down, you have no small bills for lunch money, your dog runs away, or the school's closed for a snow day. Prevention is always the best solution, but this is the real world, so have a backup plan. At a minimum, make an arrangement with your spouse or a relative, a friend, or a neighbor to step in whenever possible.

To prevent small snafus from slowing you up, try these tricks:

- Keep a petty-cash stash for lunches, field trips, bus fare, and so on.
- Always make lunches the night before (you can even make a week's worth on Sunday; most sandwich fillers freeze well). One family's rule: "Mom makes it, I take it"—that is, after his mom

packs his lunch, it's the child's responsibility to get the lunch bag from the counter and carry it to school. Get kids making their own lunch early. One reader told us her kids choose from five family food groups: "Our seven- and eight-year-olds pack a week's worth of lunches at a time. They choose one item from each food group: protein, fruit, vegetable, bread, and, of course, candy," she explains. A sample lunch might contain carrot sticks, a juice box, a cheese sandwich, and a fruit roll-up.

- Have a "morning box" or other pickup area near the door. "We have an 'Out the Door' counter where everything is put; it's the last thing you see as you go out the door," says Melanie Osley of Connecticut. She's a nurse and claims representative with two kids, ages three and eight.

Last but not least, send kids off with a warm good-bye ritual, whether it's a simple wave as they board the bus or a kiss/hug/rub-noses routine at the door of their child-care center. This provides a last element of connection before you go about your day and helps kids handle transition times better.

Working Moms' Worst Nightmares

When your child wakes up ill, school closes unexpectedly, or your child-care arrangement breaks down . . . here's what to try.

- Confer with your spouse: Can one of you stay home today? What if you stay home until noon, and then your husband comes home to relieve you?
- If you aren't married or your partner isn't available, can you call on your mother, your sister, or a stay-at-home mom in your neighborhood for help?
- Does your employer, or do child-care centers or family child-care homes in your area, offer backup care or care for mildly ill kids?

Find out *before* you need their services and make sure you've preregistered, if that's necessary. For help finding a program, call Child Care Aware at 1-800-424-2246.

- Work from home today.

4:00 P.M.

The After-School Merry-Go-Round

BEING THE WORKING mom of an infant or a preschooler is easy, say moms of grade-schoolers. With a little one, you make one trip from home to child care and that's it—your child is safe and happy for the day. Bigger kids mean bigger logistical headaches, with after-school hours to fill and activities to manage. What's a busy mother to do?

First, don't overschedule kids with activities. Some extended daycare or after-school programs offer one-stop shopping, with time for play, homework, and enrichment activities (karate, soccer, science and math clubs, and more). Others will provide transportation to off-site activities. Either of these options is often your best bet. If such a program isn't available, have kids choose one or two activities per school year or season, depending on the time commitment involved.

Three ways to solve transportation headaches:

- Team up with other parents in a carpool. Find someone who's available early in the afternoon to drop kids off at practice or Scouts, and then you can pick up the kids afterward.
- Check with your human resources department at work and find out if alternate work arrangements are available. Can you go flextime, arriving at work extra early one or two days a week and then leaving early? Or can you work from home, which would allow you to take short breaks for drop-off and pickup runs? Even if an official policy isn't on the books, you may be able to create your own program. Submit a written proposal to your boss, outlining how the arrangement would work, and ask for a trial run. (See Chapter 14 for more details on this.)
- Hire a responsible teenager or college student to provide trans-

portation and care for a few hours a day, a few times a week. Ask friends and neighbors for recommendations and check with local colleges, especially in the elementary education department.

Whatever your pickup responsibilities, share them with your partner whenever possible, especially if you must make more than one stop. "My husband and I are each responsible for one child," says Lisa Yee of Orlando, whose six-year-old attends an after-care program at school and whose toddler goes to a child-care center. For maximum flexibility "we have matching car seats and diaper bags in each car since we're never sure who's picking up whom that day," says Yee, who runs a creative services company with her husband.

WORKING MOM'S WORDS OF WISDOM

"Be Honest About Your Priorities"

My top three daily priorities are my classes, kids, and homework. I know that many women would say that their kids are the top priority, but for me right now, getting to class, doing the things I need to do to ensure our future, those are as important, and often more so, than time with my kids. I don't feel as if I'm neglecting them, because they know that when Mom gets through with college, we'll have the things that they want as well. College is a family effort, and they understand that. Friday nights I close the books and we spend our time together. By the end of the week, I'm tired of looking at schoolwork, and I know that they miss me as well, so we set up a few movies, pop some popcorn, and snuggle down on the floor with our blankets for movie night.

—**Jean Burris,** *full-time student and single mother of three school-age children*

The Flextime Option

If you crave more daylight time with your family, yet still want or need to work full-time, consider an early-bird flextime arrangement. Shift your hours so that instead of putting in your workday from nine to five, you do it from six to two or seven to three. Your company wins because you can provide extended coverage (especially good if you need to talk to staff or clients in different time zones) and you'll produce more when you have fewer interruptions. You win because you can get up and out of the house quickly in the morning (you'll have fewer interruptions, since other members of the family may still be sleeping), your commute time may be shorter (you'll be traveling outside of peak hours), and you'll be more productive at work. Your family wins because you can focus on them in the late afternoons.

To set up a flextime plan, check with your human resources department to see if there is a formal policy. If not, create a written proposal outlining what you'd like to do and why it would benefit your employer. Suggest a trial period for testing the arrangement, with a follow-up evaluation of how it's working. For more on this, see Chapter 14 in the work section.

- Of all flexible scheduling arrangements, flextime is the most common, according to a 1997 survey by Hewitt and Associates.
- Fifty-two percent of companies offer flextime work schedules, according to a 1998 Buck Consultants survey of 1,058 employers.
- Thirty-five percent of companies considering nontraditional work arrangements in the future are looking at flextime, according to the Buck survey.

6:30 P.M.

The Family Meal

WITH TWO, THREE, four, or more busy schedules to accommodate, it can be hard to corral everyone at one time for a meal. But it can be done. Once everyone begins to gather at home, take a few minutes to reconnect. Instead of immediately launching into dinner preparations, spend a few minutes cuddling on the couch or playing with the kids in the backyard. It only takes a few minutes of attention to keep kids on their best (okay, better) behavior through the evening.

Surprising Stats

Contrary to popular belief, dual-career families do eat dinner together most nights. Some 82 percent of *Working Mother* readers say they dine together at least four times a week, according to our survey of two thousand moms; 48 percent have dinner together every night.

You may also find that it's better to feed the kids first. This doesn't mean you can't still share a meal together. "We try to feed our baby first—then he sits with us in his high chair playing while we eat," says California mom and sales rep Virginia Reese Coles. For preschoolers and up, a snack usually does the trick. "Give your little ones some nutritious snacks to munch on at the dining-room table while you are cooking. They get very hungry and unmanageable then, so it's best to engage them and feed them at the same time," says Sarah Wines, an urban planner from Maryland with two children.

Even if you use these strategies, it still helps to keep dinner plans as simple as possible. Keep your expectations low. One mom found that merely calling the meal "supper" versus "dinner" took the pressure off.

"Do not be elaborate!" advises Rhona Kannon, mom to two gradeschoolers. "Plan simple but balanced meals. Keep it to what everyone likes to eat. Your menu may not vary much, but you'll have fewer arguments and a calmer, more fun evening," says Kannon, a systems developer from New York.

Keeping things simple not only speeds up the process, it also saves on cleanup time. "When my fiancé moved in, he was great about having dinner on the table every night, but he left a disaster in his wake. I didn't have time to clean the piles of dishes left behind, and his meals often took so long that dinner was late. Finally, I sat down and talked to him about it, and his meals slowly have taken on a more modest appearance, and the piles of dishes have shrunk to far more reasonable levels," says mother of three Jean Burris.

One way to minimize work is to invest some up-front time and create a meal plan. "I made up four weeks' worth of menus, with grocery lists for each week," says mother of one Michelle Schmitz, a government agent from Virginia. "Now, instead of spending time each week deciding on meals and figuring out ingredients, I just print a copy of a weekly menu and the corresponding grocery list."

A less ambitious variation on this is to plan a week's worth of meals at a time. "I do all my grocery shopping on Saturday, and I post the week's meals on the refrigerator. My husband gets things going, and I finish when I walk in the door at 6:45," says Kimberly Klein Cauthorn of Houston, who's the assistant dean at a law school and mom to three kids, ages two, seven, and eight.

Of course, the easiest way to prepare a meal is not to cook it at all. Try:

- Take-out meals—there are plenty of nutritious options out there. Anyway, no one ever died from eating pizza once a week.
- Precooked or prepared items from your supermarket, embellished with your own touches. Try adding Dijon mustard, ham, and tomatoes to deli potato salad, for example. Or whip up a fried-chicken salad by combining bite-sized pieces of chicken with a package of frozen corn (thaw under hot running water), packaged, prewashed salad greens, a cup of precooked black beans or black-eyed peas, some tomatoes, and store-bought ranch dressing.
- Forming a supper club with four or five neighbors, friends, or

relatives. Each night, one club member cooks enough food for all member families and delivers it to their homes. Everyone gets a home-cooked meal each night, but only cooks once.

- Loading up on leftovers: "Always cook more than you will need so that you can either freeze some of it, plan to have it for your own lunch the next day at work, or have the leftovers another night in the week," counsels Melinda Laughon, a Virginia mom of two. Another mom makes a game of it. "One night a week we have Restaurant Night. I take orders from the kids like in a restaurant; the menu is made up of leftovers," explains Michelle Skipworth of California, a public safety dispatcher with four young kids.
- Enlisting the help of a spouse and older children. Kids age six and up can be responsible for simple meals such as sandwiches and salads made from precut veggies. By about age ten, kids can use the stove to heat up soup or boil pasta. Cookbooks to try: *My First Cookbook* by Rena Coyle; *Someone's in the Kitchen with Mommy* by Elaine Magee, MPH, RD; *Pretend Soup* by Mollie Katzen; and *Kids Are Cookin'* by Karen Brown.

Connie Pizarro, the banker from New Jersey, employs many of these strategies to cover a week's worth of meals. "On Sunday, I cook for Sunday, Monday and Tuesday. On Monday, I cook for Wednesday. My husband is responsible for Thursday, Friday, and Saturday—he can either cook or get us take-out."

It helps to have a basic repertoire of seven or eight meals that everyone likes. You can prepare them without much thought and you know to always keep the ingredients for them on hand. "We barbecue at lot—even if it is snowing or raining," says Mindi Brenner. "My husband also does a lot of the prep work, such as cutting up the veggies, so I just have to throw them into the pot to steam or broil."

There's plenty that kids can do to help, too. Even two- and three-year-olds often love to wash vegetables, tear lettuce, sprinkle cheese, or put bread in a basket. "I also have the kids set the table and clean up after themselves. These simple tasks save me lots of time and offer the kids ways to learn responsibility and proper table-setting," says Melinda Laughon, whose son and daughter are three and five.

Make the Meal Special

While there's no need to kill yourself creating a gourmet meal, there are ways to make the dinner hour a loving family time. Limit interruptions from the telephone and television by letting the answering machine pick up calls and switching off the set. Make a smooth transition from playtime to dinner by having children help in the kitchen, make a centerpiece for the table, or take turns saying grace. A premeal ritual, such as a prayer, gets you off to the right start.

Nothing sours a sweet meal faster than a battle over an unfinished plate of food. You'll save yourself a lot of headaches if you refuse to engage in these food struggles. Require that children have one taste of an unfamiliar dish, and that's it; offer simple backups (yogurt, cereal, fruit) if kids don't like what they've been served. And never underestimate the power of humor: "Last weekend I told my daughter that if she ate her vegetables I'd go outside and crow like a rooster. She did and I crowed. Hey, whatever it takes!" says Lisa Yee.

It's tough for little ones to stay seated at the table after they've finished, so don't belabor this point. Or try Tina Lustig's strategy. "I try to prepare a complete dinner for the kids (including dessert, which is fruit) on their plates so they don't lose interest or decide to leave the table before dinner is really over," says Lustig, a software manager who lives in California with her husband and their two children, ages three and six.

A lovely way to end the evening meal is to real aloud for five or ten minutes before you begin the cleanup. And as with everything else, don't shoulder the entire cleanup responsibility yourself. As Melinda Laughon found, even preschoolers can carry their dishes to the sink; they can also wipe off tables and counters, and some are fascinated by brooms and mops. Many couples divide the labor so that whoever does not cook cleans up.

7:30 P.M.

No-Headache Homework

IF YOUR CHILD is enrolled in an after-school program, she may have the opportunity to do her homework there. If so, great! But make sure you check her work, both to make sure she's done her best and to show her that it's important to you.

If your child does his work at home, provide a quiet, well-lit environment. Many families find that the kitchen or dining-room table works best, so kids aren't distracted by toys in their room and parents can supervise easily. The television should never be on during homework time; in fact, many *Working Mother* readers tell us they ban TV altogether during the week.

To keep her ten-year-old son on track, Cathy Wright-Eger of West Lafayette, Indiana, encourages him to take frequent breaks. "We do homework in half-hour periods. Then it doesn't seem so long," says Wright-Eger, the head swim coach at Purdue University.

Linda Bookey finds that offering her two kids some autonomy works. "My son picked the time he wants to do his homework. His favorite time is in the morning instead of TV," explains Bookey, who lives in Washington with her boys.

Even if your children are too little for homework, set the scene for the future with quiet time, as Maura Fraley does. "We don't have homework yet, but each evening we make a half to one hour of quiet time for reading or catching up on paperwork to get the habit started in our child," says Fraley, a school computer assistant from Wisconsin and mother of a seven-year-old girl.

Other strategies for hassle-free homework:

- Talk to the teacher. At the beginning of the school year, find out what the homework policy is—how frequently it is assigned, how long it should take to complete, and what your level of involvement should be. You'll certainly quiz your child on spelling words or lend a hand when he's stumped by a tricky math problem, but experts agree that as a rule, kids should be responsible for doing their work and getting it done on time.

- Make a homework box: To avoid procrastination and time wasted tracking down the tools she needs for a project, make a homework box for your child. Stock it with pencils, pens, erasers, rulers, scissors, markers, a stapler, paper clips, plain and lined paper. "It makes a child feel competent and powerful to have everything on hand," says Ellen Klavan, author of *Taming the Homework Monster: How to Make Homework a Positive Learning Experience for Your Child.*
- Minimize frustration: The best way to empower kids when they get discouraged is to stay positive and offer lots of encouragement. Instead of saying something like "Come on, now. Let's get this done!" try saying "I know this is hard, but I know you've done work this hard before. You can do it." Research shows that this approach boosts kids' confidence levels and makes them feel capable of tackling even the most difficult assignments.

8:30 P.M.

Off to Sleep

WHEN IT COMES to bedtime, kids need a consistent routine—such as snack, bath, story, bed—in order to make the transition from waking to sleep, day to night, today to tomorrow. "To a child, sleep represents a kind of deprivation—the loss of her parents' company, the loss of playtime. A bedtime ritual helps offset her sense of loss by providing her with something she craves: a half hour or so of undivided attention from Mom and Dad. And, by ending her day on a happy note and associating bedtime with positive experiences, she can drift towards sleep secure in the knowledge of her family's love," says Tamara Eberlein, author of *Sleep: How to Teach Your Child to Sleep Like a Baby.*

Don't wait until children say they are tired to begin bedtime prep—that may be too late. Instead, start the routine at the same time each night. Reevaluate bedtimes once a year, say, on the child's birthday or, better yet, at the beginning of the new school year.

It's best to keep the routine to calm, quiet activities. "Start calming the kids down after dinner. This is a hard concept for my husband to grasp, but a necessity," says Lisa Yee, the mom of two and creative services director from Orlando. The experts agree: "Reserve the hour before bedtime for quiet play. This lowers your child's activity level and prepares his nervous system for relaxation. Roughhousing, running, and tickling games make the transition to sleep especially difficult," says Charles E. Schaefer, Ph.D., director of the Better Sleep Center at Fairleigh Dickinson University in Hackensack, New Jersey. It also helps to give children a five- or ten-minute warning before starting the first item on the bedtime agenda: "In five minutes, it's time to get in the tub."

Look at bedtime as an opportunity for cozy, one-on-one time with your children. "I alternate with my husband. One of us takes bedtime duty; the other does the dishes and has the rest of the night off," says Cinta Burgos, an engineer from Boston and mother of one. Many parents find that bedtime chats are the most revealing of any they have with their children.

Your routine will probably evolve naturally. Just make sure to fit in all the key components—snack, story, bath, pajamas, brushing teeth,

WORKING MOM'S WORDS OF WISDOM

"We Love Our Good-Night Ritual"

During the school year, the boys are called to snack time at eight P.M. They eat a snack of their choosing while I read to them. The picture books of old have been replaced by harder chapter books, usually something a bit above their own reading level. In the past year I have read things such as *The Hobbit, The Black Stallion, Treasure Island,* and *A Wrinkle In Time.*

After finishing their snack, the boys go upstairs, brush their teeth, change into PJs and get into bed with a book. We come in to kiss them good night and make sure their alarms are set. Then it is lights-out and we rarely hear from the guys again until morning.

—**Diane Ginther,** *human resources manager with two sons, ages eight and eleven* bathroom visit, etc.—in a consistent order. Remember to allow for some snuggle time. Set aside at least thirty minutes so you won't have to rush.

If kids fight at bedtime, take away privileges that are part of the routine, such as story time. Make a rule that dillydallying means the process will begin earlier the next day. Couch it, though, so that bed itself is not a punishment, or kids will do all they can to avoid it. Instead say, "Since it took us so long to get ready for bed, we'll have to start earlier tomorrow night. That means you'll have to miss *Rug Rats.*"

Set up a cutoff time after which there are no more snacks, drinks, trips to the bathroom, and so on. As mother of two Connie Pizarro says, "All water drinking, aches, and pains must be resolved by nine P.M."

Rachel Gould seeks to accentuate the positive. "I think it is hard for children to say good night to a good day, so we try to emphasize what the next day has in store. We might say to our son, 'Tomorrow is Thursday and Daddy has a ballgame,' or 'Tomorrow is Friday, our special day for Mom and Trey,'" says Gould, a technical writer who lives in Alabama.

9:45 P.M.

The Paper Chase

ONCE THE CHILDREN are in bed, snuggle up with a good . . . checkbook? If laundry doesn't overwhelm your home, papers and bills just might. To keep your household running smoothly (read: with less stress), it's crucial to have a system in place to track, file, and eliminate paperwork. "Keeping good records not only helps you find key documents quickly, it also saves time and eliminates headaches," says organizing expert and author Tara Aronson.

"The first step to peaceful coexistence with papers is to set up a home office area," says professional organizer Michelle Passoff. It doesn't necessarily need to be in a room of its own; you can put a desk and filing cabinet or box in a basement, hallway, or corner. Keep the area fully stocked with folders, labels, pens and pencils, scissors, tape, and a stapler.

Invest in a good file cabinet or pretty box. Spend some time organizing the file drawers so that they're most helpful to you. As you file, ask yourself two questions: Do I really need to keep this, or can I get it again if I need it? and Where will I look to find this?

Organizer Michelle Passoff recommends sorting most papers into three categories (and then subdividing within these areas):

1. **Financial/business affairs papers.** Receipts; credit-card and bank statements; investment-retirement documents; real-estate documents; insurance papers; tax returns; frequent-flyer club statements; warranties and instruction manuals; important records such as wills, passports, and birth certificates.
2. **Professional papers.** Résumés; professional certifications; articles on your industry; materials related to professional membership organizations; background for job searches.
3. **Personal-project papers.** Information on travel and vacations; background on collections you keep, classes you want to take, restaurants you want to visit.

Use the tried-and-true handle-it-once method: As you go through mail and school notices, take the appropriate action on each one immediately (note the event on the calendar, RSVP for the party, etc.). Then file—or better yet, toss out—the document. (Try this at work, too.)

Tara Aronson also recommends creating a "hot spot" for bills and other items that require attention pronto. "Use a basket, wire box, or desktop hanging file that's convenient for you and stashed where the kids can't get to it," says Aronson. "Budget ten minutes each morning or evening to go through the pile and tackle the single most pressing item inside."

Set up a system for paying bills: Plan to write checks twice a month, or create a bills-to-pay folder or tray with deadlines marked. Better yet, use automatic payments whenever a company offers this service, and sign up for electronic banking. This allows you to arrange payment with a few clicks of the mouse—even telling the bank to pay the bill in a few days or weeks. There's no more writing checks or licking stamps.

6

Getting a Handle on Housework

Mention the dreaded word *housework* to working moms and you'll hear groans and sighs in reply, and then wishes and dreams: "What I'd really like is for family members to think as if they were in charge of home management and do things like add to the grocery list, replace the toilet-paper roll, mow the grass when it needs it, and supervise our youngest child according to rules and guidelines," says Laura Aird of Illinois, a program manager with two teenagers and a seven-year-old.

Virginia mom Michelle Schmitz faces reality. "I wish fairies would come and make my house sparkle," says Schmitz, a government investigator with a two-year-old son. "But until those fairies get to work, my house will just have to perpetually stay on that narrow, cluttered border somewhere between cleanliness and filth."

The Big Picture

Before you work on improving your efficiency on individual jobs and chores, take a look at the big picture. How can you change your home, your family, and your routines to minimize housework?

- Prioritize your tasks—and then do them efficiently.
- Streamline your home by reducing clutter.
- If you have a partner, make sure he's pulling his weight.
- Get kids involved, too.

Find the Easy Way

"**S**tart by rethinking your definition of *clean,*" says household expert Tara Aronson. "Sure, Mom may have vacuumed and polished every day, but you don't have to. For day-to-day living, don't sweat the small stuff."

As with everything else, take care of first things first: "We have priority areas: Bedroom floors, kitchen counters, the dining-room table, bathrooms, doorways, and stairs must stay clean," says New Hampshire software engineer Janet Chamberlain.

To reserve some free fun-time on the weekends, "do your cleaning in spurts during the week instead of all on the weekend," advises Aronson. "Break down big jobs, such as cleaning the bathroom, into smaller tasks: Wipe down the sink now; clean the bathtub and mop the floor later." Take advantage of short windows of time to complete these minitasks. You can, for example, fold laundry or give the toilet a quick scrub while you supervise children who are splashing in the bathtub. Save yourself extra steps by keeping cleaning products in the room where they're used—but out of kids' reach.

When it comes to housework, "I use two common project-management techniques: parallel tasks and avoiding bottlenecks," says Joan Damico. She's a marketing services manager and mother of two from New York who's obviously figured out how to apply lessons learned at work to home. Explains Damico: "Parallel tasks means, for example, that while I give the children baths, my husband cleans the kitchen. The result is that more can be accomplished in less time. Common bottlenecks to avoid include: leaving the clean dishes in the dishwasher and living out of a laundry basket."

An Ounce of Prevention

- Have people remove shoes before coming in the house, or get a good doormat.
- Banish food from the family room, living room, kids' bedrooms—everywhere but the kitchen and dining room.
- When you have little children, opt for fabrics and furnishings that hide stains and dirt.

Clutter Control

Paring down your possessions saves on cleaning, upkeep, and storage. People who master organization are more likely to say they are successful, productive, and happy, according to a survey sponsored by Day-Timer, the time-management company.

Eliminating clutter can truly improve your mental health. Managing your space frees up your time—and your mind. "When things are more organized, you waste less time on frustrations," says professional organizer Gloria Schaaf. "You may save just a few minutes a day, but the real benefit is that you have a feeling of control over your environment." If you keep order, you don't waste time looking for things that are buried in a pile of unnecessary items—or dreading the inevitable big cleanup. "Straighten the room when you're in it for five minutes or more," advises registered nurse Jenny Elliott of Pennsylvania, a mother of two. "Use baskets to get items back into the rooms they belong in."

Remember two basic principles, says organization guru Barbara Hemphill, author of *Taming the Paper Tiger*: First, if you've forgotten you have it, or if you can't find it, it's of no value. Second, put like things together.

Fight the emotional-attachment trap, advises Schaaf. You may be saving old college notebooks because they represent past achievements, or an obsolete computer because it once cost a lot of money. If you can tease out these ties and talk yourself out of them, you'll be rewarded with more storage space for things you really do need.

Five Quick Ways to Gain More Space

1. Take advantage of unused storage areas like the spaces over doors and under beds and stairs.
2. Use space savers such as shower caddies and extra shelves in kitchen cabinets (go crazy at the housewares store—you'll be amazed at all the nifty gadgets they have).
3. Choose furniture with built-in storage space (don't forget about large trunks or benches with hinged seats).
4. Every time you bring something into the house, get rid of something.
5. Throw away anything that you haven't used in a year or two (seasonal/holiday items and family heirlooms don't count).

WORKING MOM'S WORDS OF WISDOM

"Clear Out Clutter Regularly"

Organize your surroundings! I take our clothes to a consignment shop twice each year. If the kids have outgrown it, or don't like it, it's out of here. Forget the hand-me-downs; it is not worth it. I go to Goodwill whenever I know I will be in the area. If an item is not being eaten, played with, read, or worn, it's out of here. This is such a relief. It's very uplifting to feel that you have done the best you could with the items you have. Now that I'm on a roll, the family offers up their unwanted and unneeded items. It feels good to help others and it's a good example.

—**Michele D. Marrie,** *financial manager and mother of three*

Give That Man a Mop!

It's obvious that offloading some of the work will reduce your household burden. What's less obvious is how you can accomplish this; getting a partner to do his share of the household chores is a major sticking point for many families. While some men pitch in gladly from the beginning, others must be nagged, wheedled, or at the very least reminded to take some responsibility. A recent *Working Mother* time-management survey found that husbands do only about 24 percent of household chores.

"In most of the couples we know, the woman does not work outside the home and the man usually has a fairly high-powered job where he is traveling a lot or otherwise unavailable," says mother of two Lori Hultin. "The wives of these men think my husband is wonderful because he helps so much. In comparison, he does, but what they don't realize is that he has to do more because I work, too! My pet peeve is that after the kids are tended to, my husband will sit down and read the paper or watch TV while I run around trying to get laundry done, countertops washed, beds made, and so on," continues Hultin, a self-employed marketing consultant from California. "Sometimes I envy the fact that he can relax whereas I feel that if I don't do these tasks they won't get done!"

How do men keep the division of household labor unequal? They're smart enough to know that they can't simply plead the 'that's women's work' excuse," says Francine Deutsch, a professor of psychology at Mount Holyoke College who studied equal parenting in a research project sponsored by the National Science Foundation. After extensive interviews with more than four hundred couples, Deutsch and her collaborators identified five subtle strategies men use to evade housework.

1. **Passive resistance.** "When I asked one father how he responded to his wife's entreaties, he answered, 'In one ear, and out the others,' " writes Deutsch in her study report, *Halving It All: How Equally Shared Parenting Works.* Forms of passive resistance can include ignoring a wife's request for help, being oblivious to chil-

dren's needs, or performing a request but doing it grumpily and grudgingly.

2. **Incompetence.** Even little kids know this tactic—if you break enough dishes, you won't be asked to wash them anymore.
3. **Praise.** "Praise at home may have the insidious effect of keeping the work within the women's domain," says Deutsch. The unspoken message is: "You're so good at it, you should do it."
4. **Different standards.** In this case, men use different—lower—standards at home. They don't care as much if the clothes are clean or the kids take healthy lunches to school.
5. **Denial.** This takes a variety of forms, says Deutsch: "Men exaggerate their own contributions by comparing themselves to previous generations, attribute greater contributions of their wives to their wives' personalities or preferences, and obscure who's doing what by invoking rules and patterns that sound fair and equal" but in practice are not.

How do you get over these hurdles? It takes work, says Deutsch. "Equally sharing mothers are an assertive crew. They communicate in a clear and direct manner, and use whatever clout they have to elicit their husbands' cooperation," she says. Deutsch concedes, though, that the women who succeed here have particularly receptive husbands. "The strength and assertiveness of the equally sharing mothers is matched by the sense of fairness evident in the behavior of the equally sharing fathers."

There's no magic bullet to solve this problem, but here are the strategies we've found to be most effective.

- **Make sure dads have extended time alone with kids** (what one mom called "forced bonding"). This helps them see just what it takes to care for a child and run a home. In one extreme case, a mom reported that when she had to leave home for six months for a work assignment, it transformed her husband (who, by the way, is a surgeon in training who must put in long hours). Now he notices and takes action when the family needs milk or diapers.

  Another mom had a similar experience. "When we had our first child, my husband worked the weekends and I worked during the week. He adjusted beautifully and continues to value and appreciate taking care of the children and helping to keep the house in order," says Shelly Whitlock-Pope, a payroll manager from New York with three children, ages three, seven, and eight.

Of course, you probably won't go to these lengths. But you can still leave your partner in charge while you take an evening out alone, a day-long excursion with friends, even a weekend trip.

- **Don't criticize his efforts.** Let him complete tasks as he sees fit. Remind yourself that the end result is what matters—a happy baby, a reasonably clean floor. You may have to bite your tongue at first, but it's worth it.

  "The best thing I learned as we became more equal was to let him take responsibility," says Wendy Ann Postlethwaite, mother of three. "That means no nagging, no directions, no micromanaging. If he is feeding the kids, it is up to him to cook/clean/choose healthy alternatives. He's an adult and if he decides to take them out instead of eat leftovers, that's okay," continues Postlethwaite, who lives in Massachusetts and works as a marketing consultant (alongside her husband).
- **Divide responsibilities based on your interests and competencies.** If you like cleaning but hate grocery shopping, do what Rebecca Hill does: "My husband is in charge of food—buying, cooking, packing lunches. I do all the cleaning. We like this arrangement because we both do the tasks we prefer," says Hill, the managing director of a foundation in New York City and the mother of a two- and a five-year-old.

  Of course, getting him to stick to the plan isn't always easy. Open lines of communication and a deep sense of respect are critical ingredients, but so is a sense of humor. Ilyssa Esgar-DeCasperis, a lawyer and mother of two from Staten Island, New York, couches her reminders in jokes: "I say, 'You know, the Board of Health called today and said that they were condemning the bathroom for unsanitary conditions, dear.' The bathroom gets done soon thereafter."
- **Discuss responsibilities—and trade thank-yous—at family meetings.** Even when progress is slow, a formal acknowledgment of everyone's effort is important. "Having monthly family meet-

ings helps because we compliment each other and talk about problems," says Katie Sleigh, a Kansas teacher and mother of two preschoolers. These meetings are also the time to plan fun family outings to reinforce the fact that you're working together as a team so that you'll have the time to enjoy each other's company.

- **Get a housekeeper or cleaning service.** A weekly or biweekly blitz by an experienced cleaner can do wonders for your mental health—and that's worth the fifty or seventy-five dollars it might cost you. Remember that your time is valuable. Many *Working Mother* readers say hiring out the housecleaning has saved their marriage!

  Also consider half-sessions (an interim clean every other week, full clean other times). If you do this, you'll pay for a full cleaning three times a month, but still have someone coming in every single week. If you live in a colder climate, you may be able to afford more frequent cleanings in the summer, when you're not paying high heating bills—and when the house tends to get messier anyway.

Bring the Kids on Board

Even if you're blessed with a fabulous housekeeper and a truly participating spouse, take advantage of another source of help: your children. You can always use an extra pair of hands, and it's critical to show kids that they're an important part of the family team and therefore need to participate in household chores. Plus, they need to learn the basics—one day they'll have their own home to keep clean. "Doing chores helps the children feel they belong and are needed—that they are a valuable (and competent) part of the family," says Nick Stinnett, a professor of human development and family studies at the University of Alabama and coresearcher of the Strong Families Study, a twenty-year project examining the characteristics of stable families. He adds that even though kids may complain about doing the tasks at the time, they're still getting a positive message.

The key here is to start kids early—when they think it's fun! At first, include them in what you're doing. For example, have them match socks while you fold a load of laundry. When they do their own chores, begin with short, manageable tasks. Use visual reminders (draw pictures or cut photos from magazines).

Ten Chores a Preschooler Can Do

1. Dress him- or herself
2. Sort laundry
3. Pick up toys
4. Empty small trash baskets
5. Mist houseplants
6. Sweep stairs with handheld vacuum or small brush and dustpan
7. Gather clippings while you weed
8. Dust furniture that's within reach
9. Feed pets
10. Put newspapers, plastic, and cans in recycling bins

Still, as kids grow, the joy of helping with chores just so they can do what Mommy or Daddy is doing may wear off. To overcome this, Myrna Shure, Ph.D., a psychologist and author of *Raising a Thinking Child,* suggests talking to kids about what they'd most like to do. When they participate in the decision-making process, they're more likely to follow through.

Working Mother readers have lots of different motivational strategies. Most say they don't tie allowance to chores—instead, chores are a required part of being a member of the family. "My children do regular chores, no allowance. My eldest, eight years old, would and does try to attach monetary significance to every little thing if given the chance," says Jeanmarie Nielsen, a Nebraska college professor. Instead, "two times a year, we have 'money-earning week' for the chores they normally do. They use the money for our vacation in July and for Christmas shopping in December."

Other strategies:

- "My kids do a number of chores equal to their age," says Mary Kay Eisert-Wlodarczyk, an architect, air force officer, and mother of four, who lives in Alabama.
- "My children have chores, but if they do things without being asked, then they earn stickers. For every ten stickers they earn a few dollars," writes Latresa Bray, a teacher and mother of two, from Columbus, Ohio.
- "I pay for my kids' camps, lessons, and activities in return for scheduled chores," says Brenda Baumgartner, a public relations manager from Idaho Falls, Idaho, and the mother of five children—including two sets of twins.
- "My seven-year-old gets seven dollars a week as long as she keeps her room clean (we took a picture of what we mean by 'clean'), makes her bed, and makes sure all of her things are put where they belong. She can do extra chores to earn extra dollars. My three-year-old loves to vacuum and sweep and mop, and he's good at putting things where they belong—especially dirty clothes into the hamper. It can be a great game, and it's a good way to have some laughs. We often play music while we do chores, and dance and sing," says Rebecca Downey, a career coach from Bryan, Texas. Many mothers agree with Downey: Chores can be "quality time." Says Jeanmarie Nielsen, "Some of our greatest talks are when we're one-on-one in a thorough room-cleaning. Normally, the kids are responsible for keeping their rooms picked up, but a few times each year we go through all dresser drawers and shelves to sort worn-out and outgrown clothes, toys, or books. We call it 'Keep or Give.' Those are great conversations."

New York City mom Lorraine Duffy Merkl says that doing chores together is an important part of her children's education. "Life isn't all playing in the park. We're busy people and have things to do. When my children come shopping or do chores with me they are meeting people in our neighborhood and learning where our food comes from and how our clothes get clean. We talk and laugh along the way—you can do that anywhere," says Merkl, a freelance copywriter and mother of two children under the age of four.

WORKING MOM'S WORDS OF WISDOM

"Think Positive"

I like to think of the windows as a way of saving my children's fingerprints forever! . . . Actually, I clean them in the spring and fall.

—**Janet Chamberlain,** *software engineer and mother of two*

Super Shopping

One thing about kids—they'll eat you out of house and home. Finding a way to shop efficiently is a must. You don't want to spend more time at the supermarket than you do in your own living room. So get familiar with your local warehouse club and keep your home well stocked with its bounty. You needn't go more than once a month, if that, and these trips can actually make a fun family outing.

For the supermarket, limit yourself to one trip a week (instead of Saturday mornings, consider going after kids are asleep on a weeknight, when the store is less crowded). Supplement with milk and fresh produce runs as needed.

Streamline your visits by knowing your needs well and planning your meals in advance. You tend to buy the same items over and over, so create a master list (one clever trick is to list items in the order they appear in the aisles at your favorite supermarket), make multiple copies, and post where everyone can see it. Simply check things off as you discover you need them.

At a minimum, keep a running list each week. "An important rule in our house is, if you use up the last of anything, put it on the list. I cannot be responsible for every item if I am not using every item. My husband and daughter are pretty good about it by now," says Donna Hawkins, an administrative assistant from Pennsylvania.

Better yet, skip grocery shopping altogether by using an online shopping service such as Peapod (www.peapod.com), Webvan (www.

webvan.com), or Netgrocer (www.netgrocer.com). Peapod takes your order online, then dispatches a shopper to your local market and delivers the goods to you—any day of the week, whatever time you choose. Webvan supplies groceries, gourmet and organic food, household sundries, even home office supplies, wine, and prepared meals to San Francisco area residents. It plans to expand its service area over the next couple of years. Netgrocer sells nonperishables only but offers discount prices. The company sends your order via Federal Express (although you won't get it overnight) and charges $2.99 for orders up to $50, $4.99 for orders over $50.

Lighten Your Laundry Load

The task of doing laundry is never-ending. "Sometimes I wonder if my neighbors aren't secretly dropping theirs off at my house!" says Ilyssa Esgar-DeCasperis. To keep it from overwhelming you, do it regularly—don't let it all pile up for the weekend. Experienced working mom Michele Marrie has two good tips: First, she recommends keeping a basket, not a hamper, in each child's room. "There is no point going the extra step of emptying the hamper into a basket," says Marrie, a financial manager with three kids.

Second, she says, "Do not have your washer and dryer in the basement if possible. Have them on the kitchen-level floor. That way, you can ask the kids to help you fold while you are cooking." This strategy also reduces the number of treks up and down the stairs you'll make each time you do a load, saving precious time and energy.

| 7 |

Weekends

Have your weekends gotten away from you? Do you find yourself just as tired on Sunday night as you were on Friday afternoon—not refreshed and invigorated from two days of family fun but worn out from forty-eight hours of errands, chores, and paperwork? If so, it's time to take action. These two days are precious. Learn how to use them to your advantage.

To help you rebalance your weekend time, this chapter provides you with, first, an attitude adjustment—a reminder to prioritize and reserve some room for fun. Second, we've got plenty of time-saving tips to help you keep must-do's from taking over.

No More "Working" Weekends

Downsize your expectations. Must you run all those errands, or can you split them with your spouse, sister, or neighbor? Do you really need to replant the flower bed by the side of the house *today*—or can it wait? Must your kids join two baseball teams and take an art class? Do you *have* to finish that report for work, or can it wait until Monday?

Find a balance that works for you: enough errands and housework to keep the house running and to catch up from last week or get a jump on next week; a few family activities; some cozy time alone with your spouse.

Error-Free Errands

Minimize your time in the car by grouping nearby errands together, reducing repeat trips, and being well prepared. "I keep a good calendar that includes a general to-do list, and I also keep running lists for the grocery store, discount store, and so on," reports Abby Marks-Beale of Connecticut, a self-employed educational consultant and speaker with two young children.

You've got it made if your company is one of the small but growing number of companies that offers free concierge services. For a small fee, a hired helper will drop off and pick up your dry cleaning, address party invitations, wait in your home for a repair person, or do anything else you ask. If this service isn't available in your workplace, it may be in your community. Or, hire your older child or a neighbor's responsible teen to do some of these tasks.

To save time, "Develop good relationships with all your neighborhood service people—a pharmacist who goes out of her way to help or an accommodating dry cleaner, for example," says New York mom Erika Muller, a project leader for a technology firm. "These people can make your life infinitely easier if you take the time to get to know them and form a bond."

Muller prefers to leave her six- and nine-year-old kids at home while she makes her rounds. "I made arrangements to pay my neighbor to watch my children every Saturday for a few hours. This way, I can get my errands done quickly and then spend time with them," she says. If you're alone in the car, you might make the tasks more pleasant by playing music that you like (instead of Raffi or Barney!) or listening to books on tape. Or see how many errands you can do on foot, and you'll boost your exercise quotient for the day.

Alternatively, you might enjoy taking a special helper with you for some one-on-one time. "Now that my five-year-old has a little sister, I think we both consider any outings together as special, quality time, even if we are just by ourselves doing the grocery shopping or running errands," says California mom Lori Hultin.

Taming Kids' Schedules

As with everything else, be sure to *prioritize.* If you don't keep the brakes on, sports practices, playdates, parties, and lessons can quickly overwhelm your weekends. Children don't want to be run ragged any more than you do. If they adore athletics or dance, fine; if they don't, there's no need for them to be signed up for lots of sports and lessons just because their friends are. Help them figure out what activities are most rewarding and have them stick to those. You might also consider limiting them to one major sport or extracurricular class per season. (See "The After-School Merry-Go-Round," page 36.)

Carpooling is critical. There's no reason for you to ferry your children to every practice when other kids in your neighborhood or along your route are going in the same direction. Use those career-building networking skills to organize an efficient carpooling team.

Birthday parties can be another sore spot. With many schools requiring kids to invite all their classmates to their celebrations, you can easily end up with dozens of parties to go to if you have more than one child. Step in to help your child prioritize. She doesn't need to attend every party—only those of her closest playmates. Manage gift buying by keeping a stockpile of appropriate presents at home. Shorten wrapping time by using (and reusing) gift bags; your children can even make a supply by coloring, stamping, and stickering plain white or brown bags.

Communicate with your spouse to make sure you've got your bases covered (see "The Family Calendar" on page 22). Teamwork is the name of the game.

Making Time to Donate Time

Community service is often the first thing to go when you're trying to balance work, home, and family—especially if your children are very young. If that's a fact for you, don't feel guilty about it. You can always resume volunteer activities in a few years, when your children are more self-sufficient.

If you do decide to volunteer, be selective and set limits. "I choose projects that have a definite end," says New Jersey mother Connie Pizarro. "For example, Women's Day at church: Once the day is over, your job is done."

"Rather than saying no when asked to help out, I've learned to be clear about the extent of my involvement," says career consultant Nancy Collamer. "I've found people really appreciate your willingness to help out and often have a way of dividing up a big task so that you can play an important role without being overwhelmed."

See Chapter 20 for more information on how to become more involved in your community.

Don't Forget to Have Fun!

Most families say that they must work hard to preserve family time during busy weekends. Many confine chores and housework to Saturdays while reserving Sundays for family fun. "Sunday is our 'wild card,' do-whatever-sounds-fun day," notes Lorri Cardwell Casey, a writer and mother of three from Arkansas. Other couples keep Friday or Saturday night sacrosanct—as date night. Try lining up a regular baby-sitter for this outing, or finding two who'll alternate.

Look for fun that's simple and laid-back. There's no need for lavish entertaining or draining trips to faraway amusement parks (except once in a while). Take a cue from Texas law school dean and mom of three Kimberly Klein Cauthorn: "We go out every Friday night to a family-friendly, inexpensive restaurant. We try to meet friends almost every week, so no one has to cook, the kids can play, and we can visit."

Lisa Jorgenson, an engineer from Minnesota, recently hit on a winning idea: "We bought two bikes and a dual trailer for the girls. It has been a great way for the whole family to spend uninterrupted time together; my husband and I have time to talk, and we get exercise, too!"

8

Special Family Occasions

Travel, Birthdays, and Holidays

As much as we talk up the value of everyday fun, we know the wonder of special times, too: vacations, birthdays, and holidays. As with everything else, though, these occasions can often seem like more work than they're worth. Read on for ways to minimize hassle and maximize fun.

On the Road Again

WHETHER IT'S A quick weekend trip or two full weeks at the beach, you're sure to take your kids on a family vacation at some point. Here's how to keep prep work from keeping you at home.

Step One: Good Planning

Think about what kind of vacation suits your family best. Travel expert Christine Loomis, the author of *Simplify Family Travel,* advises you to consider which of the following categories most appeals:

- **Relaxing:** the beach; a lakeside cabin; a condo with pool in a familiar town (translation: no reason to sightsee).
- **Action:** hiking, biking, rafting, horseback riding, tennis, golf, skiing. This can point you toward a particular geographic area or a specific camp, clinic, or course.
- **Learning:** Civil War battlefields, an archeological dig, nature studies, language immersion.
- **Sightseeing:** the Rocky Mountains, historic homes, a theme park.
- **Reunions:** an organized, weekend-long gathering; a day at Grandma's house.
- **Variety:** some combination of the above.

You'll also need to think about what you want to *avoid* in a vacation, says Loomis. This might include:

- **Making arrangements.** Maybe you thrive on the thrill of tracking down the best bargain or quickest route from A to B. But if you don't, plan on picking one destination and staying put, or—better yet—enlist the aid of a travel agent as you plan.
- **Driving with kids.** If the squabbling and constant stops make vacations miserable, avoid them. Either don't drive or take preventative measures to keep kids' behavior up to snuff (see "En Route" on page 68).
- **Breaking the Bank.** "The bottom line is that you'll want to feel comfortable with whatever trade-offs you make between the money you spend and the enjoyment you receive," says Loomis. "That may mean adjusting the definition of your dream vacation, but it shouldn't mean giving it up completely."

Use these outlines as a starting point. If your children are old enough (elementary-school age and up), involve them in the planning.

You might narrow down your choices to two or three, for example, then allow the kids to help make the final decision. Or, if your destination is a done deal—you're tacking a vacation onto a business meeting or you've got a wedding to attend—talk to your kids about what special activities they might like to do during the trip. Allow each family member to choose one activity for the whole family to do, suggests Loomis. When children feel they have a say in what's happening, they'll be much more cooperative.

Step Two: Prepping

Make a master pretrip list of things to pack and do (such as feed or board animals, lock windows, stop newspaper delivery). Post the list a week before the trip and have family members get to work, checking off each item as you go. Refine this list with each trip, adding new items and subtracting unnecessary ones, and reuse it each time.

Keep a bag of travel-size toiletries packed all the time, replenishing as needed. Then just toss it in your suitcase before you go. You can even apply this to your entire vacation wardrobe, if you do special things like skiing or camping. One mom reports that her family keeps a whole box full of camping clothes. After each camp-out, they just wash those items and then store them with the tents and other equipment. Then they're all ready for their next trip.

Make kids (preschoolers and up) responsible for one small backpack or bag. Little ones can simply carry a few toys; older kids can handle their own books and clothes. Have them pack the bag a day or two early and practice carrying it, says Loomis; they may change their minds about how much they've brought. Consider also the plastic-bag method: Pack an entire outfit in a large zip-close freezer bag so kids can dress themselves easily.

Perfect Packing

Here are five fabulous tips from travel writer Christine Loomis. Most of these apply to both children and adults.

- Think dark: Take clothing that doesn't show stains.
- Choose a color scheme and select clothes accordingly.
- Pick layer-ables and separates over one-piece items.
- Reduce wrinkle worry by relying on knits, fleece, and rayon items.
- Bring one outfit that's designated for days you're likely to get dirty.

Step Three: En Route

Keep kids occupied with plenty of activities, songs, and snacks. If you're traveling by plane, order a special children's meal if it's available. Consider purchasing some inexpensive toys, books, or travel-friendly games for the trip—novelty will buy you a lot of time. Stop often to stretch little legs. "Try not to ask kids to go from one confined space (a car) to another (a sit-down restaurant) when traveling," says Christine Loomis. "Instead, choose a picnic area, a restaurant with outdoor seating or play spaces, or a family restaurant where no one will mind if kids constantly get up and down."

For the five-and-under set, it's best to stick to normal routines whenever possible. Bring along a supply of familiar foods if they won't be available on the road or once you reach your destination. Plan your schedule to allow time and space for naps and a consistent bedtime.

On-the-Go Toys and Activities

Infants/toddlers: Chewable rattles and toys, board books, a plastic mirror, toys that attach to a car seat
Preschoolers: Magnetic board with shapes and letters, washable markers, kiddie tape player with headphones, books
School-age kids: Travel activity books, magnetic travel games, washable markers or colored pencils, personal tape player
Teens: Personal tape or CD player, books and magazines, playing cards

Step Four: At Your Destination

Go at your child's pace. Try rising early to visit tourist spots while the day is still cool and most other sightseers are still in bed or sipping their coffee. Then you can cruise back to your hotel or home base by early afternoon for naps and a swim. Never underestimate the power of a motel with a pool!

Take advantage of kids' camps or other child-centered activities if your hotel offers them. Many feature fun trips or arts-and-crafts projects related to the region you're visiting. This gives parents some R&R and time alone and keeps family togetherness from becoming stifling.

Limit arguments with acquisitive school-agers by giving them a vacation allowance. Give them free rein with it. You may have to bite your tongue to keep from commenting about their purchases, but make sure they know that when they've exhausted their stash, that's it.

Step Five: Home Sweet Home

On your return, allow yourself some decompression time. For weekend trips, don't drag in at 11 P.M.; if you'll be gone for a week or more, try to come back on Friday or Saturday. Or take an extra day off in between your vacation and your first day back at work. This way you'll have plenty of time to tackle the laundry, restock the fridge, and scan the mail.

You're Away, the Kids Are Home

Whether it's a business trip or a much-needed getaway with your spouse, leaving town without kids in tow has its own set of problems. To keep everything shipshape while you're away:

- Leave detailed instructions and contact information for your caregiver and/or for your partner, if he'll be doing chores he usually doesn't do (you can reuse these instructions the next time you go away). Sure, you may resent the fact that your mate even needs these reminders. But keeping him informed is much better than worrying about what he might forget while you're gone. When you come home, he may have a renewed appreciation for all that you do. One mom reported being impressed with how smoothly her husband kept the household running while she was gone. "Then I found out he took half days off from work all week!"
- Talk with your kids before you go away about where you'll be and for how long. A preschooler needs only a few days' notice; tell an older child further in advance. You may want to look at a map or read stories about your destination together. On a calendar, show your kids how long you'll be gone.
- Have your kids help you pick out a special memento or photograph of them to take with you on your trip.
- While you're away, telephone home at regular times so kids can await your call. Explain before you go that you'll call each night at bedtime, for example, or in the mornings before school. You might also leave notes, pictures, or inexpensive gifts for your kids to open while you're away.
- Be aware that kids might not always greet you joyously upon your return. They may be angry at you for leaving or unsure of whether you'll go away again. These feelings should dissipate after a day or two.

Birthday Bashes

IN THESE DAYS of elaborate parties featuring pony rides and backyard laser tag complete with costumes, what's a working mom to do? Keep the *Working Mother* rules of thumb in mind: Examine your attitude, prioritize, and then organize. Parties are supposed to be fun! Young children, especially, will never remember the cake you stayed up past midnight to ice or the party favors you painstakingly created during a week's worth of lunch hours.

You're perfectly entitled to limit celebrations to family, if you prefer. You might, for example, have a special daylong family activity instead of a party. If you do schedule a bash for friends and classmates, there are ways to do it without losing sleep, quitting your job, or breaking the bank. "Remember, it's your child you're trying to impress, not your friends, family, or the mothers of the other children at the party," says family management expert Kathy Peel.

First of all, you may be able to buy a great party. Establishments from gyms to hair salons to restaurants to zoos now welcome parties and will do most of the work for you—for a price. It may be worth it to you to pay that price, so all you'll do on the big day is sit back and enjoy (and take lots of pictures).

If you do opt for a do-it-yourself party, make it a family project. Team up to brainstorm ideas for themes, decorations, snacks, and games (or pore over a party-idea book, such as *The Penny Whistle Birthday Party Book* by Meredith Brokaw and Annie Gilbar, or *Birthday Parties for Kids! Creative Party Ideas Your Kids and Their Friends Will Love* by Penny Warner). Then join forces to label and stamp envelopes, assemble decorations, and fill goody bags. Break up the work into several small jobs and spread them out over a few weeks.

Four Sources for Mail-Order Party Goods

- Oriental Trading Company: 1-800-327-9678; www.oriental.com
- Paradise Products: 510-524-8300; www.partymaster.com
- U.S. Toy Company: 1-800-255-6124; www.constplay.com
- M & N International: 1-800-479-2043; www.MNInternational.com

Keep the party simple. The children will be hyped up as it is, on excitement and sugar. A good rule of thumb is to invite one guest per year in your kid's age, plus one; so for her fourth birthday, invite five of your child's pals. Limit the party to one to two hours for kids up to four years old, three hours for five and up.

Keep activities simple. Toddlers don't need any special games. Just let them play together—outside, if you can. For older kids, have an arrival activity ready (such as a craft project or simply free play). Once all the children have arrived, and they're growing tired of the first activity, move into your games or entertainment. Always have a few backup ideas in case the planned activities flop!

Follow with food. Pizza is always appropriate—or schedule a late-afternoon party and skip right to the cake and ice cream. Once the little ones are sated, you can move into gift opening. Distribute favors at the same time so that guests don't feel left out while the birthday kid collects his loot. Finally, plan a winding-down activity, such as board games or a video.

Holiday Celebrations

WHEN *WORKING MOTHER* surveyed its readers a few years ago about their holiday survival tips, we received, overwhelmingly, two responses: Simplify your celebration and plan ahead. Busy moms, determined to enjoy the spirit of the season, found that they could do just that, as long as they kept their expectations in check and their focus on fun.

QUICK BIRTHDAY PARTY REFERENCE GUIDE

Child's Age	1–2	3–4	5–8	9–12
Number of guests	2–3	4–5	6–10	11–14; or 1 or 2 for a special outing such as a baseball game
Length of party	1-1½ hours	1-1½ hours	1½-2 hours	2–3 hours
Theme ideas	Not needed	**Beach/pool* (use sprinkler and/or wading pool) **Arts and crafts* (have several activity stations set up; serve colorful foods or decorate-it-yourself cupcakes)	**Circus* (hire a clown to entertain; do face painting; serve popcorn) **Arts and crafts* (have guests make their own favors, such as T-shirts or picture frames)	**Child's favorite sport* (get appropriate decorations and cake; play game in yard or at nearby gym) **Hot movie* (decorate with posters; serve theme food)
Favor ideas	Not needed	Bubbles; coloring books and pens; stickers; sand bucket and shovel (for beach party)	Notebooks and cool pens or pencils; travel-size games; candy	Key chains; mini calendars; hair accessories; trading cards

Step One: Simplify the Season

With school programs, office parties, neighborhood open houses, religious services, and extended-family gatherings, the holiday season can quickly become overwhelming and exhausting. One defusing strategy is to safeguard some time for just immediate family. This gives you more opportunities to enjoy the season together and come up with your own special rituals and traditions. One mom recommended holding a family vote on which invitations to decline—but make sure your kids can keep the balloting private.

Take the opportunity to redefine old family traditions to fit your lifestyle. You don't need to do everything your parents did to feel the warmth of the season. Instead, keep some traditions and lose others. It may no longer be feasible, for example, to wait until Christmas Eve to trim the tree or to make the latkes in time for the first night of Chanukah. Or scale back: Bake traditional cookies, for example, but do three kinds instead of six or eight. If you'll be celebrating with your siblings, you might even enlist their help: One of you can bake a special dish, and another can dig out and display favorite holiday heirlooms.

Be on the lookout for opportunities for two-in-one fun: Mix celebrations with errands by shopping at your church's Christmas bazaar or driving through a lovingly decorated neighborhood during your shopping trip. Duties that once seemed like chores can be fun if you do them with someone special, so invite one child or a good friend to shop with you. Kids make ace baker's assistants: They're great at decorating gingerbread men and sugar cookies. They're also good at stuffing, labeling, and stamping greeting-card envelopes.

With so much excitement and extra fun, it's more important than ever to keep children to their regular routines whenever possible. "We try to stay on our regular sleeping and eating routines," says a mother of three from North Dakota. "We kept bedtimes close to normal last year—even if we had to leave a party early—and we found that our children were better behaved than they had been the year before that." This goes for travel, too: When kids are small, you may prefer to have relatives visit you, instead of adding the stress of travel to an already busy season.

Seven Ways to Simplify Gift Giving

1. Pare down your gift list: Allow children to ask for one "big thing" only. In your extended family, limit exchanges to children only, or draw names out of a hat.
2. Ask for wish lists from your family members. One reader told us

that she used a simple questionnaire, asking relatives to list their sizes, favorite colors, and any hobbies or collections they had.

3. Consider planning special dates or excursions instead of giving gifts. This works especially well for spouses.
4. Try a one-size-fits-all strategy: Give everyone framed photographs of your children, baked goods, crafts that are handmade by the kids, or mail-order products related to your area (such as citrus from Florida).
5. For teachers or caregivers, consider a group gift agreed upon and paid for by all the parents in the class.
6. Shop mail-order—it eliminates the need to wrap and ship gifts, or even leave your home!
7. Shop online. After you describe what you want, online shopping tools will search the Web and report back to you with prices and availability. Try these sites: www.acses.com (books); jango.excite.com and www.junglee.com (general); apparel.com, catalogsite.com (clothes); www.shopper.com (computers and electronics).

Step Two: Plan Ahead

Do not, we repeat, do not attempt to finish your holiday shopping on Christmas Eve or during the day of the first night of Chanukah. Take care of this chore early so you can concentrate on decorating, baking, entertaining, and, most of all, enjoying the season as the holidays draw near.

We've learned several great shopping strategies from *Working Mother* readers:

Buy in advance. That means year-round. Keep your eye out for those hard-to-find nighties your mother likes or special magnets for your sister-in-law's collection. Use sales to stock up on gifts for unexpected occasions. Many moms designate a special box or shelf for this booty. (You can use this strategy for birthday parties, too—see page 62.)

Shop on weeknights after kids are asleep if your husband or caregiver is available to stay with them. You can cruise in and out of stores more quickly without little helpers. An added bonus: Malls will be less crowded at these hours.

Shop by category. Devote one day or half day to gifts for men, another for women, younger kids, and so on, so you can concentrate on specialty stores. It's also useful to create a plan of attack before you go. Decide what you'd like to buy for each person on your list and where you're most likely to find it; then you can group nearby stores together.

Wrap as you buy (don't forget to label). You'll spare yourself a late-night, last-minute wrapathon. Plus, you won't have to find as many hiding places for the loot! Gift bags are a handy timesaver, but they're expensive. Instead, invest in a stash of plain bags from a party-supply store and let the kids go to town with stickers, markers, and stamps.

Likely as not, you'll still want and need to save time on other holiday projects. If you have vacation days left, now's the time to use them! Keep your kids in their regular child-care arrangements (at least for part of the day) and use that solo time to finish up shopping and wrapping, baking, cleaning, or decorating the house. Better yet, have your spouse take some time off, too, so he can pitch in. Make a day of it by treating yourself to lunch out.

Other time-saving holiday strategies:

- Make cookie dough in advance and freeze it. This breaks up your baking into two or more sessions—mixing the dough, and then rolling, decorating, and baking, as needed.
- Find out the dates of holiday parties for work and social groups or friends as early as you can. Plan for a baby-sitter if you'll need one—especially for New Year's Eve.
- After the holiday (or any gift-giving occasion), keep items to be returned in the car. That way you can make the exchange the next time you're near the store.

| PART THREE |

WORK TIME

How to Reduce the Amount of Time You Spend Working and Increase Your Productivity and Job-Effectiveness

You work for so many reasons: You enjoy the satisfaction of completing an important task. Your family depends on your income. You're passionate about the difference you make on the job. You enjoy practicing the skills you've developed, and learning new skills. You love the company of hardworking peers. You've earned an expensive college or graduate degree and want to make the best use of it.

Whether you view your work as a fulfilling career, a bill-paying job, or something in between, it does take time, time that you might otherwise spend with your family or (gasp!) pursuing personal interests. So you need to make the most of your job in the least amount of time. In this section, there are many useful strategies for maximizing the positive aspects of your job while minimizing the negative parts. We focus on:

- How to **Stop Stress** (Chapter 10) using stress-reduction techniques. You'll find removing stress from your schedule frees up extra time—and you will become a more relaxed, healthier, happier person.
- How to save time by using the best **Tools of the Trade** (Chapter 11)—everything from calendars and planners to computers, voice mail, and other technologies, plus filing and storage solutions that keep clutter under control.
- Smart ways to control your workplace environment and **Take Action** (Chapter 12). We explore alternative ways to negotiate all the nitty-gritty of your workday (except for the actual work): delegating, working efficiently, using your lunch hour to the fullest, managing business travel, exploring (and winning) alternative work options, recovering from mistakes, handling difficult coworkers, coping with interruptions, and handling overtime requests.

- What you need to know to master **Crisis Management** (Chapter 13).
- And, what you can do when you decide to say **Bye-bye, Nine to Five** (Chapter 14)—alternative work options from flextime to part-time.

| 9 |

Making Work Work for You

The working mother's prayer goes something like this: Please help me to work more efficiently, to enjoy the time I spend at work, and to leave work behind when it's time to be with my family or do what I need for myself.

It can be answered by applying the following formula:

***P**lanning + **P**rioritizing = **P**roductivity.*

Planning ahead is essential, but it's most effective if you combine it with prioritizing. You need to figure out not just what needs to be done, but when.

"I create yearly goals and I break those down into objectives or subgoals by month. Then every week, either Sunday night or Monday morning, I break the monthly goals down into clear deliverables for that week," says Pat Begrowicz, the director of process technologies for a research firm. "The greatest obstacle to getting things done is when I lose my planning time at the start of the work week—due to interruptions by coworkers mostly—because then my week gets off to a bad start. I am much more relaxed and in control when I have had my thirty-minute planning time," says Begrowicz, who lives in Ohio and has three children under the age of nine. "If I can stick with my plan at least eighty percent of the time, I feel good."

Begrowicz does everything right: She works backward from her big goals, she breaks down her projects into manageable chunks, she charts her progress, and she makes time to plan. She doesn't leave anything to chance, but she still has a healthy, realistic attitude. She knows she won't always get to everything, but she has a strategy in place that allows her to get right back on track if she's derailed for some reason.

Nobody's Perfect

At work, it's easy to slide into the perfectionist trap. After all, you want to do your best, and your supervisors and coworkers expect it of you, too. But not knowing when to say "when" is counterproductive: Once you've made your best attempt, additional hours of agonizing won't improve your final product enough to be worth it. So learn to quash your perfectionist impulses. Try these strategies:

- Develop a good-enough barometer. Enlist your boss's input to help you decide what's finished and what really does need more time and effort.
- When you find yourself devoting a disproportionate amount of time to one task, ask yourself: Is this worth it? Why am I still working on it? Are other projects suffering? Post this reminder by your desk, tape it into your planner, send it to yourself via E-mail—whatever it takes to get the message across.
- Don't overanalyze your mistakes—learn from them (see page 113).

For more ideas, see "Don't Sweat the Small Stuff" on page 13.

Determining exactly what you need to do in advance of a large project, which might include pressing your boss for detailed instructions on your task, reduces wasted effort, mistakes, and backtracking. Once you're clear on your tasks and your deadlines, you're ready to get to work. That goes for day-to-day tasks, too. Don't just do whatever's on top of your desk—do what's important. That means, of course, that you've got to *know* what's important first.

You'll also need to factor in time to manage unexpected emergencies (see "Coping with Inter . . . rup . . . tions," on page 116). Flexibility serves you well here. Knowing that you can't predict and plan for everything keeps you centered and calm. It counterbalances the control-freak impulses that can leave you feeling anxious and overwhelmed if you can't complete your tasks the way you initially set out to.

Doing your work better, faster, and smarter will help you enjoy it more. So, too, will reducing the negatives you experience on the job. Cutting down on stress, conflicts, mistakes, and work/life spillover not only makes you feel better, it also improves your productivity and efficiency. They are two sides of the same coin. Most of the strategies we'll outline in the following chapters provide the consummate opportunity to multitask: As you reduce negatives, you boost job efficiency and satisfaction.

WORKING MOM'S WORDS OF WISDOM

"Remember Your Priorities"

When bedlam prevails and I start to blow my fuse, I give myself a time-out and try to remember what the real priorities in life are. I remind myself that I work from home to afford myself flexibility in caring for my children, so if my day is interrupted by a call from the school nurse's office, I should be glad for the opportunity to pick my daughter up in five minutes rather than frustrated by the work I will miss that day.

—**Nancy Collamer,** *career consultant and mother of two girls, ages seven and ten*

Upping your efficiency at work is a boon for your family, too. Accomplishing your work tasks more effectively gives you more time for the rest of your life. It also cuts down on the ambivalence, guilt, and discord that can run over into both work and family when life gets too hectic.

Take a minute to think about what gives you the biggest thrill about your work. Is it the sense of accomplishment you get from moving up the career ladder? The joy of improving another person's life by providing support, medical care, or vital information? The comfort of opening that envelope on payday, knowing that you're making an important contribution to your family's well-being?

Once you know your goal—what matters most to you—you'll be better able to organize and prioritize at work. If your aim is to make plenty of money, then you'll want to focus on landing high-profile assignments and developing a reputation as a highly productive employee. If you have a different goal—say, you want to spend lots of time with your preschoolers but plan to pursue your career more aggressively later—then you may decide to cut back your hours but still maintain a presence in your field. Or perhaps you need to earn a full-time salary but also want some flexibility in your schedule: Then you may want to explore a flexible work arrangement, in which case you'll need to become expert at being very efficient during the time you're at work.

The nature of your job also matters. If you manage a large department or must call on lots of clients, you'll obviously have very different needs and goals than if you own a small home-based business or practice a hands-on profession, such as medicine or education. The key is to find the strategies that work best for you.

How Ambitious Are You?

Recently, we discovered that there was very little research available on the ambitions of working moms. So *Working Mother* surveyed its readers on the topic. More than 1,250 of them responded to a poll published in the magazine. The results were striking:

- Ninety-two percent of the respondents said they consider themselves "ambitious" or "highly ambitious."
- Forty-three percent of the "highly ambitious" women said the birth of their first child made them feel even more ambitious.
- Ambitious women said one of their high-priority goals was "to set a standard of achievement for my children."
- Fifty percent of the ambitious moms said they do not put in long hours, but use their time at work "creatively and efficiently." (See Chapter 12 for ideas on how to do this.)
- Thirty-five percent said they "work smarter by putting most of [their] efforts into important, highly visible assignments." (Check out "Beat the Clock-Watchers" on page 119 for more on this strategy.)

| 10 |

Stop Stress

When you're slammed with stress, you waste time because of lowered efficiency, distraction, exhaustion, and bad judgment. In addition, you can alienate your coworkers, family, and friends. And the health repercussions include lowered immune strength, heart stress, and digestive problems.

To stop stress damage to your relationships, your job performance, and your own peace of mind:

- Take stock of what *your* stressors are. Don't assume they're the same as your husband's, your best friend's, or your coworker's, advises Paul Rosch, M.D., director of the American Institute of Stress in Yonkers, New York. Your colleague may hate deadlines but love to juggle multiple projects, for example, while you have just the opposite reaction.
- Distinguish between stressors you can do something about (constant interruptions or missing information) and those you can't (an

unbudgeable deadline). You tend to feel the most negative stress when you feel a situation is out of your control. "The stress-reducing effects of having a sense of control have been demonstrated time and again in both animal and human studies," says Dr. Rosch. "If you can't fight and you can't flee, you have to learn to flow."

- Learn techniques to help you go with the flow.

Stress Test

The top three stressors reported by moms in the *Working Mother* time-management study were as follows:

- having too much to do in the time I have to do it: 77 percent
- feeling there is never time to catch up: 50 percent
- not getting enough help from my mate: 29 percent

Other strategies for coping with stress:

Get physical. Use your body. Many of the most effective stress-reducing techniques are physical in nature. Aerobic exercise (walking, running, dancing, biking, in-line skating) relaxes muscles and relieves tensions. So does soothing exercise such as yoga. When you exercise, your body produces and releases endorphins—natural mood-elevating and painkilling chemicals. Most fitness experts recommend working out at least three times a week. Recent studies show that three ten-minute sessions are just as good as thirty minutes straight—especially if the alternative is cutting out exercise altogether because you don't think you have the time for it! (For more on fitting in fitness, see Chapter 18.)

Another body-calmer is progressive muscle relaxation. With this exercise, you repeatedly clench and then release your muscles. Start with your feet and move slowly up to your head; with each muscle, squeeze and then relax. This helps your muscles "remember" the relaxed, resting state instead of the tense one brought on by stress.

Similarly, try a few simple stretches. Research conducted at the University of Kentucky has shown that stretching can help reduce muscle tension and even lower blood pressure temporarily. It doesn't much matter which muscle group you stretch, but it is important to hold the stretch for ten to thirty seconds. Pause for a minute in between stretches. Stretch gently and *do not* bounce: You could overdo it and strain—or even tear—the muscle. Plus, you're not getting the full benefit of a nice long stretch if you're bobbing up and down.

Sample stretches to try: Loosen up tense neck muscles by slowly lowering your chin to your chest; then to the left and right; then gently tilt your head back, with your chin pointed to the ceiling. Soothe sore wrists (good to do after a typing spree) by extending your arm, palm facing up in the front (as if you're motioning for someone to stop), then gently stretch it back toward your chest with your other hand. Reverse directions and point your fingertips down, then use your other hand to gently bend your hand back toward your body.

Did You Know Exercise Boosts Creativity?

British researchers asked subjects to come up with unusual uses for tin cans and cardboard boxes—before and after twenty-five minutes of aerobic exercise. The more inventive uses came from those who had pumped up their heart rate and their thought processes. (Breathe deeply!) So here's another good reason to get up from your desk and take a brisk walk!

Don't forget to breathe. Yet another simple, do-anytime-and-anywhere stress reliever is deep breathing. When you're under stress, your breathing tends to be rapid. This causes a drop in blood levels of carbon dioxide, which can lead to tiredness and anxiety, plus create muscle tension. Deep breaths increase the oxygen to your brain and body. The result? A clearer head, slower breaths, more relaxed muscles, and a calmer state of mind. Simply breathe in through your nose as deeply as you can, hold for a few seconds, then exhale slowly through your mouth. After a few normal breaths, take another deep breath.

Make up your mind. Meditation and visualization are very effective for stress relief. To meditate, simply sit in a comfortable position, breathe deeply, and focus on a soothing word or sentence, such as "I feel calm and relaxed." Repeat it to yourself, either silently or aloud. The idea is to focus your attention entirely on that simple word or phrase. Ideally, you should devote twenty to thirty minutes to this exercise, but even five minutes can help.

With visualization, the goal is to replace stressful thoughts with calming ones. As with meditation, you begin with a comfortable position and a few deep breaths. Then picture yourself in a relaxed, stress-free state. Try to use all five senses: Don't just see yourself on the beach; smell the salt, hear the surf, feel the sun's heat.

Get the kinks out. A luxurious way to relieve stress is with a massage. Whether from your partner or a pro, a nice rubdown will go a long way toward relaxing your muscles and easing your tension. When office politics have you in a tizzy, ask your spouse for a quick foot massage or back rub—and return the favor another time.

Give Yourself a Massage

There are also some massage techniques you can do without a partner. Here are a few self-massage techniques based on acupressure points in the body:

- With one hand, pinch the area between the thumb and forefinger of your other hand, which is called "the Meeting of the Valleys." This pressure point helps relieve head- and face-aches and aids in digestion.
- To alleviate eyestrain, massage your temples.
- To banish headaches and promote relaxation, massage the base of your skull with your fingertips.

Eat smart. Use your diet to combat stress. When you're racing to meet a deadline or in the middle of a high-stakes deal, stock up on complex carbohydrates (whole grains, beans, seeds, nuts, fruits, and vegetables), which increase the levels of serotonin in your brain and can help you feel more relaxed. Drink lots of water. Resist the urge to consume caffeine—it can make you jittery and interfere with your rest. Alcohol is another no-no: While you may at first feel relaxed when you drink, the effect won't last, says Dr. Rosch of the American Institute of Stress. When it wears off, you'll feel tired and possibly even depressed.

Sleep on it. Scientists still aren't sure why it is we sleep, but some believe it's a key way we relieve emotional and physical stress. "While our bodies can relax during wakefulness, our minds cannot," says Katherine A. Albert, M.D., Ph.D., author of *Get a Good Night's Sleep.* "As long as we're conscious, our sensory apparatus is continually registering information, which the brain processes."

Lack of sleep makes you grumpy and fogs your brain, making it harder for you to deal with stress. It also weakens your immune system, leaving you more susceptible to illness. "Sleep-deprivation experiments show that subjects quickly lose mental abilities when they're operating on insufficient sleep, while one study of schoolchildren found that students who were two to three years behind their peers quickly caught up when they were encouraged to get more sleep," says Dr. Albert.

Unfortunately, though of course unsurprisingly, most women get less sleep than they need. Three quarters of women ages thirty to sixty do not sleep eight or more hours per night during the workweek; 16 percent sleep less than six hours per night during the workweek, according to a 1998 survey of over one thousand women done by the National Sleep Foundation (NSF). Aside from the demands on their time, women's sleep is often disturbed by menstrual symptoms and pregnancy.

Aim for eight hours of sleep per night, says the NSF. While sleep needs vary, research shows that eight hours is the amount most adults need. You can make up lost time with naps or on weekends. If you have trouble falling asleep, though, try to keep sleep patterns consistent throughout the week. Other tips from the NSF:

- Exercise regularly, but finish your workout at least three hours before bedtime.

- Exercise may relieve some symptoms of premenstrual syndrome and increase the amount of deep sleep you get.
- In the evenings, avoid foods and drinks high in sugar and caffeine, as well as salty foods and alcohol.
- Consult your doctor, if needed. The NSF survey found that while 41 percent of women *think* they've had insomnia in the past year, 53 percent said they experienced one or more of insomnia's symptoms (difficulty in falling or remaining asleep; intermittent wakefulness; early morning awakening) often or always in the past month.

Make stress work for you. Women are more susceptible to stress, says Alice Domar, Ph.D., director of the Mind/Body Center for Women's Health at Harvard Medical School in Boston and an expert on stress. She says it's because women tend to be perfectionists—and because they don't take good enough care of themselves. "Women are so concerned about doing everything for everyone else that they end up being unable to cope with their own problems," says Domar.

Domar and other experts advise stress sufferers to take the nervous energy they're experiencing and rechannel it. "We don't want to completely avoid stress, or we'd miss out on all those wonderful high-energy chemicals that keep us alert and primed to respond. We can learn to ride that rush of hormones to greater performance, if we choose," says James E. Loehr, author of *Stress for Success: The Proven Program for Transforming Stress into Positive Energy at Work.*

How can you redirect that nervous energy?

- When you're in a high-stress period, make sure you're taking care of yourself, says Loehr: eating well, sleeping enough, exercising regularly, and making room for fun activities. "These are the things that will replenish the energy you lose during high-stress times and help you continue working at full steam," says Loehr.
- During the workday, take regular breaks from what you're doing. Scientists who study biological rhythms say your body needs a break about every ninety minutes. That means stopping what you're doing and switching to something altogether different for at least fifteen minutes.

- Adopt a new attitude. Instead of grumbling about your workload or a difficult project you've been assigned, learn to think of it as an exhilarating challenge. "You'd be surprised at how your mental and emotional state can increase or deplete your energy levels," says Loehr.

Take a reality check. When you can't seem to make time for other stress relievers, and when efforts to talk yourself out of your anxiety prove futile, is there any hope? Yes, says Allen Elkin, Ph.D., director of the Stress Management and Counseling Center in New York City. His advice: Rate the amount of stress you are feeling on a scale of 1 to 10, with 1 being slight irritation and 10 being intense panic, fear, or anger. Then rank the importance of your stressor, again from 1 (the copy machine is out of paper *again*) to 10 (you've just been fired). Compare the two numbers: are they similar? If a level 2 stressor is causing you level 8 stress, you've blown the situation way out of proportion. Ask yourself: Will I even remember this incident in a few days/months/years? This may be enough to stop your stress reaction in its tracks.

Beat Stress at Its Own Game

Do you know what people would call you if you didn't have any stress? Dead. That's right, without those biochemicals that tell us to react to stimulus or danger, we'd be goners. And we wouldn't accomplish anything that makes life interesting.

So do some mental conditioning. Instead of spending two weeks saying, "I have a speech to give and I'm so stressed out," try to get into a more positive attitude and say to yourself, "This is an exciting challenge that I know I can handle. It may be difficult but I can learn from it and it is going to strengthen me."

Think about your graduation, or wedding day, or the birth of your child. You bet they were stressful, but would you have missed out on them? Managing stress, using it to succeed, is a matter of conditioning and attitude. It's meeting a challenge with excitement, succeeding, and greeting the next challenge with a little more assurance. That's what good stress can do for you—increase your energy level and performance.

Stress-Relief Recap

Here are ten ways to ease anxiety in a few minutes—without straying far from your office:

1. Take a brisk, five-minute walk—even if it's simply a lap around the lobby or parking lot.
2. Have a healthy snack such as a piece of fruit or a slice of whole-grain bread.
3. Close your office door or escape to an unused room and run in place or do some jumping jacks.
4. Call someone you love—your child, husband, or a friend—for a quick, mood-lifting chat.
5. Take ten deep breaths.
6. Stare at a photo from your last vacation and imagine yourself back on that beach, boat, or ski slope.
7. Do some neck rolls or wrist stretches.
8. Switch on some soothing music.
9. Indulge in a fifteen-minute catnap.
10. Dozens of companies now offer on-site massage. If yours is one of them, take advantage of this perk now!

| II |

Tools of the Trade

Countless electronic gadgets and software programs promise to revolutionize your workday and make you a paragon of efficiency. Voice mail, E-mail, and computers are supposed to save time—but often seem to waste it too.

The truth is, of course, that not every tool is right for you and that you must use the ones you have properly. You get out of them what you put into them. If you don't invest some time in learning the system, it won't be working as hard for you.

Tracking Key Information

The two pillars of your time-arrangement strategy are your calendar (or scheduler or planner—whatever you prefer to call it) and your to-do list. "I use a paper-based organizational system, which I started doing about four years ago," says Ann Withington, an administrative assistant and mother of two from Maine. "It saved my life—there's a place to write down anything and everything you need to remember. It also allows for goal setting, long- and short-term."

Your Calendar

Day-Timer. Filofax. Franklin Covey. Week-at-a-Glance. A spiral-bound notebook from the drugstore. How do you figure out which paper planner is right for you? Ask yourself:

- What kind of information will I be recording? How often do I have meetings, sales calls, or deadlines to track?
- Do I want to combine personal and professional information in one place?
- Do I want something I can carry with me, or something that will be left on my desk or wall?
- How important is it to me that the planner look good?
- Do I need to synchronize my information with colleagues or a partner?
- Which of the fancy features will I truly use?

Choose the simplest planner you can. Aside from making sure it has all the essentials, such as a calendar and a to-do list, it's really a matter of preference. Remember to consider size: too small and you'll have to use a magnifying glass; too big and you won't want to lug it around everywhere. Loose-leaf systems let you add or remove pages and personalize the planner. It's also easy to fall into the trap of believing that snazzy sections and specialized pages will really get you organized. But if you won't use them, it's a waste—and more clutter, say Barbara Hemphill and Pamela Quinn Gibbard, authors of *Simplify Your Workday.*

Once you've selected a system, familiarize yourself with its features. Set aside some time to enter in the data you'll need to get started, and then you're off! Check and update the calendar often, and keep it with you whenever possible. If you're caught without it, take notes on whatever's handy—but transfer the information to your master planner as soon as possible.

Then treasure this item with your life! "Keeping this planner up to date is critical to remaining organized. If I ever lose it, things will be really ugly for a while," says California mom Christina Schwerdtfeger, an environmental scientist who keeps both work and family information and appointments in her planner. To safeguard against loss, you may want to photocopy key pages of your planner regularly (say, once a week or once a month). Or consider an electronic organizer—either handheld or on your desktop computer. These can be backed up on disk so you'll never be stuck for long.

Electronic calendars and information managers: Personal information managers, or PIMs, are an ever more common and popular alternative to paper-based systems. These software programs are even mandatory in some workplaces. If yours is one of them, be sure to learn all of your particular system's bells and whistles. You may be surprised at its power.

PIMs provide not just scheduling, but also integrated to-do lists, address books, project tracking, and expense-account organization. Most feature alarms and reminders to alert you to upcoming meetings and deadlines. If you're using an office-wide system, you can schedule and reschedule meetings for a group quickly and easily. Drag-and-drop scheduling allows you to move an appointment to a new time slot without retyping other key information.

If you deal with lots of clients or vendors, you may want to consider a contact manager program. More powerful than a PIM, a contact manager is good for keeping track of lots of people, maintaining detailed schedules, and making notes about phone calls, conversations, and other contacts. For both contact managers and PIMs, you'll need to analyze the offerings of several different programs to get a sense of which one will work best for you. Ask your MIS department for help.

Computer expert and author David Busch recommends you consider the following when choosing a PIM:

- If you're not too tech-savvy, select a PIM without tons of bells and whistles. It will still have all the basics you need (calendar, appointment scheduler/reminder, address/phone file, and so forth), and you'll waste less time and confusion trying to figure it out.
- If your work requires you to be on the phone constantly, choose

a program that has an easy-to-use phone book that lets you dial numbers automatically through your computer modem.
- If you still use a Rolodex or planner in addition to this program, look for a PIM that can print pages designed to fit inside them.
- If you do lots of business travel, look for a PIM that tracks travel expenditures—many don't offer this feature.

You can also consider a handheld electronic organizer (currently, the most popular one is the PalmPilot). Most come with a memo pad, date book, to-do list, address book, expense-report program, and calculator, and you can usually add on a "Palmtop" version of some of the programs on your desktop, such as Quicken, Excel, Act, and Outlook. You may even be able to use your handheld computer to check your E-mail, surf the Web, or receive pages. Look for an organizer that transfers information easily back and forth with your desktop machine.

Your To-Do List

One of the best organizational tools you can use at work is still the good old-fashioned list. Whether you jot it down in pencil on a legal pad, type it on your computer, or enter it into a tiny electronic organizer, a list can truly make or break your day. "List making is my big help," says Texas mom Sherrie Thornton. "When I see everything on paper I can prioritize, sequence, and even eliminate projects to fit the available time. It also helps to clear the clutter in my mind rather than carrying it all around in my head. Once it's committed to paper, I don't have to remember it anymore," says Thornton, who owns a secretarial/résumé service and also homeschools her two children.

Thornton has hit on all the advantages of this powerful tool. Why force yourself to rely on your memory? The judicious use of a list frees your mind up for other, more important work. To maximize the power of your list:

- **Use a prioritizing strategy.** Two popular methods: "urgent versus important" and ABC. With urgent versus important, you code key tasks on your list with a *U* if they are urgent, an *I* if they are important, or a *UI* if they are both. Some tasks may be neither urgent nor important, so you save those for last; do the

UI's first, then the *U*'s, then the *I*'s. Similarly, in the ABC code, *A* means the task is a "must-do," *B* means it's a "should-do," and *C* stands for "could-do."

To make the most of these strategies, you must take a hard look at your tasks—surely, not *everything* on your list is both urgent and important. Factor in deadlines, the project's visibility, and consequences of late or unfinished actions. If some items on your list depend on input from colleagues or clients, get the ball rolling on those first; while you're waiting for feedback, you can be working on something else. If you're still having trouble distinguishing the *A* tasks from the *C*'s, consult with your boss or a trusted coworker. And don't forget to delegate early and often (see page 106).

- **Be specific.** Do not list huge projects; instead, break them down into smaller, more manageable tasks. This will give you a sense of accomplishment as you achieve intermediate goals. It will also help you plan your work: If you can see all the steps laid out before you, you'll have a better idea of how much time you'll need.
- **Keep a master list.** This will help you prioritize. The master list has your overall projects and goals on it. Use it to generate a daily or weekly list with smaller tasks and goals. For more advice on list making, see Chapter 4, "Figuring Out Family Time."

But I Just Hate Lists

If you prefer a more visual system, "cover a clipboard with a sticky note for each task to do, and move the notes around for easy, instant reassessment of priorities," say Barbara Hemphill and Pamela Quinn Gibbard, authors of *Simplify Your Workday.* It's important to keep the notes in a designated place—the clipboard—*not* scattered all over your work area.

Show Your Computer Who's Boss

Your computer can save you lots of time and stress if you know how to make it work for you. It can save you from repeating your efforts (if you create a template for a frequently sent letter, for example) and help you find things quickly and easily (if you organize your files well). It can crunch numbers so you don't have to, store thousands of pages of information much more elegantly than a filing cabinet, and transmit messages in a fraction of a second. Computers are essential in running everything from air-traffic control to your local fast-food restaurant to your small home-based business, so learn to love them.

In your work, use the best tool for the job and use it well. Don't keep a long list of addresses in a word-processor file; find out how to use a simple database instead. Don't add up numbers yourself; save time and reduce mistakes by using a spreadsheet. Invest in training so you'll get the most help from your software. "Research shows that the typical user takes advantage of less than twenty percent of the capabilities of the software he or she uses," say authors Barbara Hemphill and Pamela Quinn Gibbard. Instead of groaning about "wasting" a day in a training session, look on it as an opportunity to save yourself time and headaches down the road. That one lost day is peanuts compared to the minutes and hours you'll reap later.

To keep your computer in tip-top shape:

- **Develop a system for organizing and identifying files.** Usually a setup of folders and subfolders works well. You might organize it project by project: A master folder marked JEFFRIES DEAL could contain other folders for correspondence, research, and spreadsheets. Or, store your work in chronological files. Use file names that help you identify the document instantly ("newleads.doc" or "2001bug.xls").
- **Keep your data safe.** Back up your work religiously—both on your hard drive and on a separate, removeable storage unit such as a Zip disk. Guard against viruses with virus-protection software. Clean up your files often (by deleting unneeded files and also by scanning and defragmenting your hard drive). Use a surge

suppressor or uninterruptible power supply (UPS) to protect yourself in case of power loss.

Talk to Me

Keeping in close communication with your coworkers and clients is bound to be a big part of your job, an area where organization and efficiency can make the difference between having something done and having it done *right.* "Good communication makes my job run smoothly," says Kimberly Berg, a sales manager from Michigan and mother of two. "I try to get my ideas across in an efficient manner so that when I ask people for their assistance, they understand what I want them to do and why. I'm still working on improving this; too often I find that I am taking care of a problem that was the result of miscommunication to our field people or customers."

To be effective, workplace talk needs to be:

- **Warm:** Keep conversations friendly and pleasant.
- **Specific:** Spell out exactly what you need in order to prevent misunderstandings.
- **Simple:** Include essential details, but don't clutter your request with extraneous information.
- **Direct:** Even if what you've got to say is difficult, the person you're talking to will appreciate it if you get to the point quickly.
- **Attentive:** Communication is a two-way street. Make sure you allow room for the other person to speak, and listen carefully to what she says.

The Telephone

Be prepared both to make and receive calls. Before you place a call, make sure you know what information you're seeking. Jot down a few notes if you need to. This will keep the conversation from dragging on too long. If you know the person you're calling will be chatty, set a limit from the beginning. Say something like, "I need to leave for a meeting in a few minutes, but I wanted to ask you about. . . ." If you've left a message and are awaiting a return call, keep any information you'll need in a designated spot (perhaps a folder marked WAITING FOR FEEDBACK or an On Hold tray on your desk). If you're in the middle of something and won't be able to give a caller your full attention, don't answer your phone; that's what voice mail is for (see "Coping with Inter . . . rup . . . tions," page 116).

Cellular phones can be a boon to working moms who need flexibility. "I'm required to be on call after hours about four times a month. I use a cellular phone when I'm on call so I can travel around and not be stuck at my home," says mother of two Nancy McConnell, a marketing coordinator from Iowa. Used safely and discreetly, a cell phone can keep you plugged in to your work (and your family!) when you're commuting or forced to wait somewhere like on a line at the bank or in a doctor's reception room. One mom reported that she checked in with her boss via portable phone while waiting to enroll her daughter in preschool.

Voice mail is your friend (really!). As with your computer, you need to learn how it works so you can make it work best for you. Many systems allow you to fast-forward or rewind while playing back your messages, pass them on to colleagues, leave group messages, and switch back and forth between a primary and secondary greeting. Find out what features your system offers, and use them.

If you'll be away from your phone for more than a few hours, say so in your outgoing message; then you won't have to listen to messages from repeat callers. Direct callers to an assistant or colleague, if possible.

When you play back your messages, keep track of them in a designated spot. "I have a notebook where I record all my voice-mail messages. This includes phone numbers and conversations I have on the phone. If something took place over the phone, I know where to find it," says Linda Anderman, an outreach specialist at Los Alamos National Labs in New Mexico and the single mom of a nine-year-old daughter. "If I have an action item from the phone call I make a box next to it that I can check off when completed. For meetings, I make a star in the margin."

When you're the one leaving a message, always explain the purpose of your call. Speak slowly and clearly. To reduce phone tag, leave detailed messages and *don't* ask for a response if you don't need one. Instead of saying, "I have the information you requested on the trade show—call me," say, "The trade show will be held in San Francisco on October 23 to 26 and they expect about six thousand attendees. Anna has already reserved a booth for us, and we'll have a room to display our entire spring line."

Electronic Mail

E-mail is perfect for quick exchanges of information—and especially handy if you don't like to use the phone. Even more so than voice mail, it allows you to ask a detailed question and then gives the recipient time to collect the information you need and respond quickly and succinctly.

As with voice mail, learn the ins and outs of your E-mail program so it can help you be more efficient. Find out, for example, how your program stores mail. Does it automatically keep messages you send? For how long? Can you change these settings? What about messages you receive? Can you sort them into folders you've designed yourself, so you can find them again quickly if you need them? Be sure to delete old, unnecessary messages often so that you won't clog up your system. This way, when you're searching for something you really do need, it won't take so long to find.

Your program might offer other handy tricks, such as the ability to delay the sending of a message until the time or date you specify. You might use this to send a meeting reminder. When you set up the meeting, create a reminder message that will go out the day before or the morning of the meeting. Another useful feature is filtering capability.

WORKING MOM'S WORDS OF WISDOM

"Keep It Short"

I leave messages at times when I know people will not be in. This way they can process their answers and get back to me with just the information, and not a lot of extra words.

—**Michele Marrie,** *financial manager and mother of three*

This helps you sort out urgent messages from ordinary ones or junk mail. It's also very helpful if you belong to a listserve that generates a lot of mail. You can arrange for it to be zapped right to a designated folder, then read it all at once over lunch or turn to it when you're stuck on hold.

To save your recipients time, keep your messages brief and simple and your subject headers informative. Your subject line may make all the difference if you receive a cryptic reply such as "yes" or "next Tuesday" with no reference point. Your recipient may not have copied your original message into her response, but if your subject heading is clear, you can tell from the header what you were asking about.

Red in the Face

Remember that E-mail is *not* private. Don't send anything you wouldn't write in a postcard or say to the intended recipient's face. Here's a good tip from Barbara Hemphill and Pamela Quinn Gibbard: "To guard against the embarrassment of accidentally sending a message before you've made sure it's worded the way you want, leave the address line blank until you're all done. This also helps guard against sending a message to the wrong person."

Paper, Paper Everywhere

Much more so than at home, paper can threaten to overwhelm you at work. But clearing out the clutter improves your efficiency by helping you locate important information quickly and, just as important, keeping your mind focused on the tasks at hand rather than the piles of junk all over the place. "Organizing reduces tension by helping you feel more in control of your surroundings," says Robert E. Thayer, Ph.D., a psychology professor at California State University, Long Beach, who has studied stress and moods extensively.

To keep your paper piles under control, focus on three areas: mail, filing, and projects in progress.

Mail

"Be ruthless with your incoming mail—toss as much as possible," says organizing expert and author Barbara Hemphill. Another organizing guru, Stephanie Winston, calls her system the TRAF method. For everything that comes across your desk, decide if you need to:

- Toss it,
- Refer it to someone else,
- Act on it, or
- File it.

The key is to handle incoming documents as little as possible. Don't look at the memo, sigh, and resolve to think about it later. If you really must act on it, do it now—or at least write the task onto your to-do list, then toss the memo. If you receive a lot of reports or periodicals that you need to read, put them straight into a TO READ folder. Then take that folder to the gym, flip through it during your commute, or make appointments with yourself once a week to catch up on reading.

Try stemming the tide of mail before it even gets to you. Cancel subscriptions to publications you never get around to—weekly or daily periodicals more than three weeks old aren't worth reading or saving. Cut off unnecessary memos at the source. "I had myself removed from distribution lists that I really didn't need to be a part of," says Connie Pizarro, a New Jersey bank vice president and mom of two.

If you have an assistant, train her to open your mail and filter it carefully. She should be able to handle some tasks (such as scheduling meetings or returning phone calls) generated by your mail.

Filing

As you go through your mail and find items that must be filed, mark which file they belong in—and a date they can safely be discarded, too. Then you, your assistant, or an intern can put these papers away quickly, as well as clear them out later.

Filing is one task that you *can* allow to build up a bit before you tackle it: It's easier to file things in (small!) batches rather than one by one. Rather than leaping up from your desk to file papers the second they come in, put them aside in a TO FILE folder. Just be sure to clear out this folder *often.*

The task of filing (not to mention retrieving documents) will be less onerous if you keep your drawers well organized. Allow plenty of space and keep folders clearly labeled. Keep less-used files in drawers that are hardest to get to (the bottom or top ones). Really think about what system will work best for you: A chronological arrangement, with folders for each week? Folders for each client you deal with, stored alphabetically? A drawer designated for a specific project, containing separate folders for different tasks? Whatever method works for you, take some time to set up that way *first.* This initial investment will be worth it on the day you effortlessly retrieve a piece of vital information just in time for a big meeting.

Is It Time for a Pro?

If disorganization is really hindering your efficiency at work and you can't make any headway alone, consider enlisting the services of a professional organizer. These experts help you create systems that keep your office, home, and paperwork in order—for good. They don't come cheap, but your company may be willing to cover the costs, since it's an investment that will pay big dividends in productivity.

Professional organizers (or POs) do their magic by observing you at work and analyzing the habits and misconceptions that keep you disorganized. They spot common but insidious problems—such as constant interruptions, a failure to delegate, and poor use of office space—and show you how to correct them. Your PO will also follow up with you after your new system is in place, to make sure it's still working.

To find a PO, contact your local chapter of the National Association of Professional Organizers (NAPO), or call NAPO's national office in Texas (512-206-0151). When you screen potential organizers, ask for a client list and references. You may be granting this person access to sensitive information, so she needs to be trustworthy and discreet. Also find out what the PO's specialty is—some work mostly in homes, others in businesses. Business POs may even have subspecialties, such as accounting or law.

Projects in Progress

What to do with papers associated with projects you're working on right now? Keep them handy, but don't let them get out of hand. Use the file drawer in your desk for these, or keep them in a stacking file or standing organizer on your desktop or another surface. "I keep my work in file folders according to project," says Linda Anderman. "I find multiple colors help me locate the files I need: blue is the rewards and recognition program, green is child care." You'll be looking at this stuff a lot, so choose containers that you enjoy seeing—baskets instead of wire trays, for example.

Here's a good rule of thumb of office organization from Barbara Hemphill and Pamela Quinn Gibbard:

IF YOU USE IT:	Daily	Weekly	Monthly	Less than monthly
KEEP IT:	On top of your desk	Inside your desk	In your office	In off-site storage

12

Take Action

"If it is to be, it is up to me." It's a cliché, but there's a kernel of truth in every sappy statement. There really are many proactive steps you can take to work more efficiently. We'll look at them in this chapter, discussing strategies such as delegating your work to others, scouting out trouble spots, designing your day for time-effectiveness, maxing out your lunch break, and exploring alternative work schedules.

Action #1: Delegate

Wouldn't you just love to pass off some of your work to an eager underling? Sounds great, doesn't it? Being a kind, wise authority at work (and at home) is rewarding—and helps you accomplish your job more quickly and easily.

Yet many women don't take advantage of the opportunity to delegate. That leaves them with a crushing workload. Why do they resist the chance to get help?

Some are afraid of seeming too pushy. Others feel guilty asking others to do "dirty work" or boring tasks. Still others are perfectionists or control freaks: "It'll never be right. It's just easier if I do it myself," they say. (For strategies on coping with perfectionism, see Chapter 3: "Don't Sweat the Small Stuff.") Some people are too controlling—they don't want to show that someone else can do their job. Others are short-sighted: "It'll take too long to teach her how to do it," they protest.

To beat these psychological obstacles:

- Focus on the time you'll save *after* that initial investment you're dreading.
- Remember that you are not giving up your duties. You are getting the support you need to do them *better.*
- Remember that delegating wins you a loyal staff—if you give them good opportunities to show their stuff. "One of the big reasons people leave jobs is a lack of satisfaction because their boss didn't delegate," reports one human resources expert.
- Recognize that others may do something differently but still do it well.

How do you decide what to delegate? Retain those parts of your job that require your special expertise or judgment. Keep political, policy, and personnel decisions, or things that require your boss's approval. Aim to give away jobs that aren't an efficient use of your time, but remember to mix up scut work and rewarding tasks so your staff doesn't get burned out. Match tasks with staffers' skills and preferences when possible.

Organization expert Stephanie Winston recommends making a chart:

Jobs someone else can do (or be trained to do)	Jobs that can be divided between me and someone else	Jobs only I can do

When you do assign a task to someone, be clear about what you want and when you want it. She'll appreciate the guidelines. Give background and context when appropriate: "The report I'm writing will eventually be read by the CEO, so the stats you're gathering really need to be powerful." Define all the tasks involved, and help set priorities. Afterward, review the project together. Then you'll both be ready for the next project that comes along.

No one to delegate to? Develop a delegating attitude anyway. Dream of what you'd pass on if you could. Then you'll be ready when the time comes. Lisa Yee sure is—she knows exactly what she wants. "Hiring more people who are highly motivated and self-directed would maximize my productivity. I run the creative department and saw a huge difference in productivity—both mine and the business's—when some top talent was added," says Yee, a Florida mom of two and co-owner of a creative services company.

Action #2: Check Efficiency

Along with delegating, another proactive step to help you make the most of your time is to do an efficiency check. This means taking a step back to review your work and your processes. What's slowing you down or stressing you out? How can you squeeze a little more out of your day—without feeling rushed?

Analyze how you really spend your time. Write it down—keep a

WORKING MOM'S WORDS OF WISDOM

"Be a Team Player"

My job runs smoothly because I have set expectations and objectives for my team—I work closely with my manager and my team to know what is going on so I can clearly understand the needs of my business.

—**Virginia Reese Coles,** *sales manager with a twenty-six-state territory and mother of a toddler* time diary for at least a week, tracking what you're doing in fifteen-minute increments. What patterns emerge? Are you shocked to learn, once you add it up, how much time you spend answering E-mail or walking to and from the copy machine? Is there a way to streamline these processes, say, by making only one trip per day to the copy machine or asking an assistant to make your copies?

Your time diary may expose other patterns, too. During what times of the day are you most productive? Work with your body's rhythms and with those of your officemates. Perhaps you feel most energized early in the morning, while your coworkers are still choking down a second cup of coffee. If that's the case, tackle tough projects that require concentration during this time of day. Similarly, keep a stash of mindless projects for lag times when your brain is a little more sluggish or your coworkers more noisy.

Action #3: Get Smart About Timing

Sometimes *when* you do something is just as important as *how* you do it. If you can begin to determine the optimum moment for each task that you do, you're on your way to true efficiency. Learn to appreciate *different kinds of time,* and use them to your advantage. Bobbi Linkemer and Rene Richards, business communications experts and authors of *Get Organized,* have identified the following categories:

- **Transition time** (from when you get up to when you arrive at work). "Use this time to think about what you are going to do, to create a positive mind-set toward your activities, the day, your goals, and what you want to achieve."
- **Commuting time.** Preview and plan your day. Catch up on reading if you aren't at the wheel.
- **Between-meetings time.** "Perfect for short-term planning, such as completing your to-do list for the day."
- **Waiting time.** Good for reading.
- **Quiet time.** "Schedule this time for relaxing and recharging your mental batteries so you will have the energy to focus on your priorities."

- **Contact time.** "Use this time to return telephone calls or visit clients. Schedule this time. It is one way of eliminating the interruption of telephone calls or people dropping by unexpectedly."
- **Thinking time.** "Schedule this time when you need to complete an important report, the annual budget, or strategic planning. Ask your colleagues to respect this time and make yourself available to them at another time."

WORKING MOM'S WORDS OF WISDOM

"Apply Good Work Habits to Every Situation"

Efficiency and productivity are my top priorities at work. I set a tough but realistic schedule and stick with it. It's the same way that I run my whole life.

—**Beverly Witham,** *dentist and mother of two*

Six Surefire Ways to Beat Procrastination

If you have trouble getting your work done on time, try these tips to help you overcome your inclination to put off until tomorrow what you need to do today.

1. Break down your task into smaller pieces and space it out over a few days. You may find yourself so pleased by your progress that you do more than you've planned.
2. Do one thing you don't want to do first thing in the morning—get it over with!
3. See if you can find an easier way around a dreaded task. Can you delegate the job you've been avoiding?
4. Make yourself an offbeat reminder. If you've been meaning to

file stacks of invoices for a month, dangle a nail file from your desk lamp.

5. Change your environment. Can you swap desks with a coworker, retreat to a conference room, even escape to a restaurant? This will cut down on interruptions, too.
6. Enlist a support system: Ask a coworker to check in on you or help you celebrate when you've completed a job you once put off.

For more procrastination-stoppers, see Chapter 2.

Lunch Crunch

"I savor my lunch hour and plan for it, just as I savor and plan for my weekends," says a Colorado mom of two. Here are eight super ways to spend your lunch break:

- Rendezvous with your husband for a midday date. Bonus: no baby-sitter bill.
- Visit your children at an on-site or near-site child-care center. This is especially useful for nursing moms. Consider bringing lunch to your child's caregiver, too.
- Work right through it—and go home early.
- Do errands galore: Make drop-offs and pickups at the dry cleaner, bank, and pharmacy, for example. You can even grocery shop—stores are pretty empty at midday. If you're not close enough to home to drop off your purchases before heading back to work, keep a cooler in your trunk for perishables.
- Take care of unfinished family projects: One mom sewed Halloween costumes during her lunch break; another organized her family photos into albums.
- Do some exercise. Visit the gym, run, walk, or climb stairs.
- Unwind over a relaxing lunch with friends or coworkers.
- Close your door or escape to a sunny spot and *rest.*

Working on the Road

Just when you've got everything running smoothly at work, wham! You can get thrown for a loop by a business trip. Not to worry: We've got ways to help in this department, too.

- Plan ahead. As you set your schedule for the days you'll be away, time appointments appropriately so that you don't have to rush from one to the next in an unfamiliar place. Build in cushions to account for unexpected delays, and be sure to get good directions.
- Make a checklist before you go so you won't forget anything. Save it for your next trip, too (see the section on family travel, page 67). You'll need to bring along important contact information, files, or samples to have during your meetings, and any and all accoutrements for your laptop. Also tote some healthy snacks—on most airline flights these days, you're lucky if you get a bag of pretzels to eat, and missing meals can make you feel tired and stressed out. You might also want to bring portable exercise gear or gym clothes so you can take advantage of your hotel's fitness facilities or do a miniworkout in your room. Don't forget to take along a few snapshots of the kids.
- Organize your expense-account information as you go along. Set aside an envelope just for your receipts, or designate a compartment in your briefcase, purse, or wallet for them. If your company uses a software program to track expenses, enter information as you go if possible. Or bring along the paper forms and begin completing them while you're on the road.
- For tips on keeping your home and family life in order even when you're miles away, see "You're Away, the Kids Are Home" on page 70.

13

Crisis Management

Or, How I Learned to Ice-skate in a Hurricane

Despite your best efforts at planning and prioritizing, you can hit a lot of snags in one eight-hour day. You aren't working in a vacuum. Even if you've escaped the corporate world to start your own small business, you still have to deal with other people. And—darn them—they can get in your way sometimes. In this chapter we'll discuss how to react in situations that can slow you down and waste your time. The following strategies help you jump back on track.

"Oh, No! I Made a Mistake"

When you've made an error—whether you blew off a client's call, lost an essential piece of information, or neglected to do something that was important to your boss—it's important to recover from it quickly for two reasons. First, you need to make amends so that your job isn't adversely affected. Second, you need to avoid getting mired in self-doubt and stress, which, aside from making you miserable, will keep you from moving forward or doing your job well.

If you goof up, **admit your mistake** to yourself and your superiors. We should know from the example of our politicians that a cover-up is bound to slap you in the face sooner or later. You'll win points if you take the high road—and show what you're doing to fix the problem you created.

Next, **make amends** as best you can. If you forgot to mail an important document in time, find out whether you can fax it or send it by messenger—even drive it to its destination yourself, if that's what it takes. If you've deleted an important computer file, do what you can to recover or re-create it. If you've neglected an important client, send a simple, sincere note of apology. You might even include a small gift.

Finally, **show that you won't make the same mistake again.** Analyze what went wrong. At what point could you have prevented the problem? How can you stop it next time? Once you've come up with a solution, discuss it with your boss: "I worked with Sam from the MIS department to create an automatic save feature for these key files, so we won't lose anything crucial in the future." Once you've completed these steps, you can put the mistake behind you and move on.

Work Would Be Great, If It Weren't for the People

Only the most easygoing soul could get along with everyone at work. If someone rubs you the wrong way, it could hamper your productivity—and your enjoyment of your job. If you've got a difficult coworker, you need to figure out how to get along.

Some interpersonal conflicts stem from "face time" issues or resentment of flextime or part-time arrangements. Your colleague may not realize that even though you're leaving early, you're still pulling your weight. Or she may forget that your part-time schedule comes at the expense of your paycheck. "I once had a supervisor who created long meetings that had little value, insisted on making people travel when it wasn't necessary, and found reason to gripe on just about every topic," says Michele Marrie, a financial analyst and mom of three from Maryland.

Your first step is to find out if the problem you're perceiving is really a problem. Is the coworker who's giving you a hard time singling you out, or is she just an all-around grouch? Maybe she's coping with a sick child or parent, and the stress is making her irritable.

If that's not the case, talk to a few trusted colleagues about the situation. Maybe you have done something to upset the difficult person, or maybe there's been a miscommunication. Is your boss sending the wrong signal to others in your department about what your responsibilities are? *Are* others being forced to pick up your loose ends? Marrie says that in each situation with her boss, she'd try to determine if the problem was "academic" or personal.

Once you have a sense of the background, set up a private meeting with the problem person (or people, if there's more than one, but meet with each one separately). Try to be neutral and matter-of-fact. Let the person speak without interrupting her to defend yourself. "I tried to break her arguments down into logical parts," says Marrie. "Then I asked questions about how I could solve or fix each part."

Acknowledge the troublemaker's feelings, then lay out your own case in a calm manner. Approach the situation as a problem you are trying to solve together: "How can we resolve this so we both feel better?"

As a last resort, go to your boss, *her* boss, or a union representative. Perhaps she can set the record straight about your hours or responsibilities, or encourage the person you're having trouble with to act in a more professional manner. But don't be a tattletale. Explain what you've already done to try to ease the conflict, and then ask for more help. Don't just dump the problem in someone else's lap and expect her to make everything better.

Or you can resolve to rise above it. "Once you are in a no-win situation," says Marrie, "don't make excuses for why the person is the way she is." Coworkers may tire of needling you if you don't give them the satisfaction of becoming annoyed. Another ploy: Act the part until you aren't acting anymore. For example, if you must deal with irate customers or vendors: Pretend to be exceedingly polite until it becomes a natural response.

Coping with Inter . . . rup . . . tions

"I'm interrupted constantly. It's stressful, knowing I have something to do and can't get it done. It's hard to balance what's more important—because everything is!" says one mother of two, an account manager for a dental office in New York.

Yes, interruptions are a frustrating fact of life in most workplaces. Why are we faced with so many of them?

- Technology means everyone wants a quicker response. We're expected to answer ringing phones, beeping pagers, and constantly incoming E-mail right away—there's no "it's in the mail" leeway.
- Team structures, now common in many workplaces, mean less time alone, less privacy, and fewer closed doors.
- Space crunches and efforts to save on real-estate costs mean there often aren't doors to close in the first place.
- Moms grow used to interruptions. Kids, especially babies, demand instant attention, so dropping what you're doing to deal with them becomes a habit that carries over into the workplace. "The interruptions themselves begin to feel routine," says a cardiovascular technician and mother of two from Pennsylvania.
- You may even interrupt *yourself* if you're bored with the task you're working on or anxious about how you will do.

So how can you protect yourself when you're hit with a series of interruptions? First, it may help to appreciate what's *good* about being interrupted: It makes you feel needed, for one thing, and it prevents boredom. Imagine if you sat behind your desk all day, every day, and never spoke to a soul? You'd be ready for a few interruptions then, no doubt.

Interruptions can also recharge you through distraction. In one experiment, being interrupted to work on something else ended up *helping* people who were at an impasse with the first problem they were asked to solve. "Often, when you return from an interruption, you'll have a spurt of great progress because your pattern of thinking will have changed," says psychologist Andrew Patrick, Ph.D., of Ottawa, who conducted the research.

Still, thinking good thoughts can only get you so far. Other strategies for interruption-prone days:

- Recognize what you've accomplished during the interruption. You may even want to write it on your to-do list: "Give missing figures to Angela," "Help Dave with computer problem."
- Find a back-on-track strategy. This may mean making a mark where you left off when going over a document or column of figures, for example, or having a written plan for work. You can quickly see where you need to dive back in if you've got a running list of what you're trying to accomplish.
- Don't underestimate the time you'll have to devote to resolving interruptions—that is, don't assume you'll have large blocks of time to complete a project.

If you're in the middle of something urgent and you must avoid interruptions at all cost, you have three options: ignore the interruption, negotiate with the interrupter, or hide.

Ignoring the interruption takes strength. If it's the phone that's bugging you, switch off the ringer if you can. You might even cover the message indicator light so you won't be tempted to drop what you're doing and see who just called. If it's a person you're trying to discourage, use body language: Don't face him fully; keep your eyes on your computer screen or whatever task you're occupied with. "If I'm on the phone and people come to my door, I don't look up," says one mom. "If I make eye contact, they'll continue to try to get my attention."

If you must acknowledge the person who is trying to interrupt you, negotiate: "I'd love to help you with that, but right now I really need to finish what I'm doing. Can you wait half an hour?" Stress that you're happy to help, just not right now.

Still being pestered? Reach for the last trick in the bag: Hide. Scout out an unused office or conference room where you can have some peace and quiet. Or ask if you can work from home—provided you have good child care, it's often the best way to accomplish a task that requires some serious concentration.

Stopping Insistent Interrupters

The telephone:

- Use that voice mail! That's why you have it.
- Does your office phone have Caller ID? Many systems will tell you whether the call is in-house or not; this can help you determine whether you must pick it up.
- Leave detailed messages to reduce callbacks (see "Talk to Me," page 99), or send E-mail.
- When you return calls, cluster them together.

Coworkers:

- Help them help themselves (this works for kids, too!). If you're chronically being asked where to find something or how the computer program works, perhaps you need to take some time out to give some additional training.
- Ask drop-in visitors how much time they need; if it's more than a few minutes, ask if you can set up an appointment instead. Let them know from the start that you're in the middle of something.
- Have a ready supply of tactful "Nice to see you, now get lost" lines. For example: "Thanks for stopping by. I wish I had more time to chat, but I need to finish this up by five," or "I'd love to hear more about this. I'll call you later this afternoon."
- Don't keep any extra chairs in your area, or keep them covered with stuff.
- Don't sit facing the door—then you can use body language to show you're busy.
- If anyone stays too long, give him something to do: "Oh, I'm glad you're here. You can help me collate this thousand-page report."

"Can You Stay Late?"

It's another one of those working-mom nightmares: Your boss asks you to stay late to finish up an important project, but you've got to pick up your kid from child care. How can you get out of this sticky situation?

Prevention is important here: Give an advance warning before a situation like this crops up. Let your boss know that you can't be available after a certain time unless you can plan for child-care alternatives. If you're then asked to stay late, remind your boss of your conversation and promise to stay late another time instead. Better yet, come up with another solution: Say, "I'd love to help you finish that, but I need to pick up my son at six o'clock sharp. I'd be happy to crunch those numbers at home tonight or come in early tomorrow morning."

You create goodwill by being a hard worker when you are in the office and by being willing to be flexible and pitch in whenever you can, either by arranging with your spouse to stay late one night per week, skipping lunch during crunch times, or taking work home.

Find out what your caregiver's policies are. Maybe she *can* take care of your child after hours as long as you give her a certain amount of notice or pay an extra fee. Know your company's policy, too: a few progressive ones, such as Xerox, Prudential, and Sara Lee, will reimburse you for additional costs incurred for overtime child care.

Whatever the options, you need to have a backup plan in place well in advance: an agreement with your partner, a promise to trade favors with a neighbor, or an understanding relative who's available in a pinch. Situations like these are yet another reminder that all working moms need a support network they can count on.

Beat the Clock-Watchers

For many moms, being asked to stay late once in a while is a minor matter. The bigger issue at many companies: a reliance on face time, the perception that if you leave right on time or work a flexible schedule you must not be productive or serious about your job. "Many managers still think if they can see your face, you're productive," says Marcia Brumit

Kropf, vice president at Catalyst, a research and advisory firm devoted to women in business. "That's not true, of course. Just being there doesn't mean someone is productive."

But if your boss—or her bosses—feel this way, how can you get ahead, or even stay afloat? How can you be visible and valuable while still arriving on time for child-care pickups and dinner preparation?

There *are* strategies for success:

- **Strive for irreplaceability.** Develop a skill or specialty that no one else has. Or take on projects that others don't want to do. By doing this, "I am developing a reputation as the one you can count on," says Toni Thompson, an occupational therapist and mother of two from Florida. Another approach: Volunteer for committees or company-wide projects that make you known to other departments. The goal is to buffer you from the misconception that you're not pulling your weight because you leave on time or work flextime.
- **Show your stuff.** Your best efforts will come to nothing if no one's aware of them. "I never really used to strut my stuff," says Thompson. "Now I make it a point to talk up the committees I'm on and the projects I'm doing."
- **Target your efforts for maximum impact.** Figure out your company's main priority and make it yours, too, even if you see your contribution as small. "It's critically important to sit down with your manager and have clear objectives," says Joy Bunson, senior vice president of organizational development at Chase Manhattan Bank in New York. "Once you can focus on outcome, face time is less important."
- **Work hard.** Make it obvious that when you're at work, you're efficient and driven. Keep socializing to a minimum, and issue reminders that your time is precious. "I let my coworkers know that I do have deadlines," says Tanya Mahoney, a fund-raiser from Texas. "If there is a project looming, I let them know that I am not to be bothered, that my immediate project is the task of the day."
- **Discuss your schedule with your supervisor.** If you're going against your company's style by scooting out the door at five

o'clock on the nose, or coming in late and then shortening your lunch hour, talk with your boss about it. "It's important to have an open conversation with your boss," says Marcia Kropf of Catalyst. "You might say, 'I know the standard schedule is to be here at eight-thirty, not nine, but that isn't working for me. I don't want you to think I'm late because I don't care. I want to be a good performer, and I'm hoping that we can come up with a mutually agreeable solution.' "

- **Make technology work for you.** Cell phones, voice mail, E-mail, and conference calls help you stay on top of business that must be done after you leave the office.

14

Bye-Bye, Nine to Five

Exploring Alternative Work Arrangements

Even the most efficient working mom may find that her work hours just don't jibe with her family's needs. Perhaps you'd like one day a week to volunteer at your child's preschool. Or maybe your commute is too long, cutting severely into your family time. Maybe you'd like to be at home to meet your kids after school.

The solution may lie in an alternative work option such as flextime, telecommuting, a part-time position, or job sharing. "I cut back to working only three days a week. This allows me a happy medium," says Judith Ercolini, a Massachusetts paralegal and mom of two preschoolers. "Sure, we don't have as much money, but the trade-off of spending more time with my girls is well worth it. I am grateful that my employer has allowed me this flexibility. In the future, when my kids are in school, I hope to change to five shortened days a week. Eventually, I will return to work full-time. With the constant changes in my field and technology, I feel it is important for me to be at least part-time. I wouldn't dream of not working," says Ercolini.

Flextime

Flextime, an increasingly popular and available benefit, allows employees to shift their schedules so that they put in a full day, but not necessarily during regular, nine-to-five hours. A mom who wants to be home when her preteen son gets home from school might arrive at work at 6:30 A.M., for example, and leave by 2:30. This allows her to earn a full-time paycheck and still be available for her son after school. These early-bird shifts are especially popular: "We've found that when a company institutes flextime, the early shifts are always the first to fill up," says Charles Rodgers of the Boston-based work/family consulting firm WFD. "People would much rather get their day started at seven A.M. than come to work at ten A.M. They prefer to have more time at the end of the day."

Many companies are now offering flextime, recognizing that it costs little and reaps big benefits. About 75 percent of U.S. employers surveyed in 1997 by Hewitt Associates offer it. "Companies that treat employees well and earn reputations as great places to work make more money, period," says Bill Catlette, a human resources consultant in Collierville, Tennessee, and coauthor of *Contented Cows Give Better Milk.* Catlette and coauthor Richard Hadden scrutinized ten years' worth of financial records of dozens of companies, then compared a cross-section of firms that are famous for nurturing a healthy work/life balance against some of their competitors. The family-friendly companies produced nearly twice as much net income—or profits—as their less friendly competitors.

Variants of flextime include **daily flex,** where an employee may change her hours daily to best suit her schedule, and **midday flex,** which enables workers to take extra time off during the middle of the day in exchange for an earlier start or later end to the day. Another similar program is the **compressed workweek,** in which employees complete forty hours of work in four days, giving them the fifth day off (or eighty hours of week in nine days, with the tenth day free).

Telecommuting

Also known as **flexplace,** telecommuting is the option to work from home anywhere from one day a week to full-time. Most often, a telecommuter comes to the office three to four days a week, then puts in the remaining one to two days from home. Or she may put in a half day at the office, then work the rest of the day from home. Telecommuting does not eliminate the need for child care—it's hard to concentrate on work when your baby is crying, your two-year-old has lost a favorite toy, or your seven-year-old insists on showing you a bug he just found. Still, it reduces time and money spent on traveling to and from work, and for many moms that's very valuable.

Company policy on telecommuting varies. Some employers foot the bill for a complete home-based office; others require the telecommuting employee to purchase her own computer and/or other necessary equipment, such as a fax machine or an additional phone line. Telecommuting isn't for everyone, nor does it work with every kind of job, especially if it's done full-time. It can be isolating. But the relative solitude and quiet of the home are energizing for many working moms.

Part-Time

As Judith Ercolini found, part-time work can be a boon for working moms who want to keep one foot in the office and one foot at home. Melissa Newman, an administrative assistant and mother of two from Texas, finds she's quite productive on a part-time schedule: "My hours coincide with the school day. Although my employer would love for me to be full-time, they've had a hard time finding long-term employees for this position. I am able to complete a similar workload in my time compared to my full-time counterparts, so it's a win-win situation."

If you want to work part-time, you'll have to assess the financial and career penalties you may incur. If you carry your family's benefits, you may have to pay a prorated fee for them, depending on the hours you work each week.

Job Sharing

What if you'd love to work part-time, but your supervisor balks, saying he needs you all forty hours a week? Or what if the nature of your work requires that someone be present in the office full-time? Then consider a job share. A variation of part-time, it's a division of a full-time job between two part-time employees.

Job sharers must be excellent communicators and, it nearly goes without saying, very compatible with each other. Picking the right partner is the all-important first step. To find one, look for someone whose work style is similar to yours and someone you know you can trust and depend on. Scour your contacts in the company and in your industry. A few large firms even have job-sharing databanks or matching services, where human resource department staffers help those interested in job sharing find each other.

Once you've got a partner, you need to develop a plan to get your job share off the ground and then to keep it running smoothly. Lori Weiss Kost, the mother of twin toddlers, shares a position as marketing and promotions director at a publishing company with another mom of twins. Kost works Monday through Wednesday; her partner, Kathleen O'Neill, covers Thursday and Friday. Kost identifies the following steps to job-sharing success:

1. **Find an ally.** Look for someone who believes in you, your abilities, and the importance of work/life balance; someone who's willing to go to bat for you and is influential at your company. In Kost's case, this was her boss, who had previously seen a job share work at another company. "She was more than willing to give us a chance and to present our proposal favorably to the company's management," says Kost.
2. **Have a strong track record.** "It helps if you've already been working at the company and have built relationships, as well as proven your abilities and skills," says Kost.
3. **Have a clear vision.** Outline—first for yourself, then for your supervisors—how you see your job-share arrangement working.

Be sure to spell out how the company would benefit from accepting your plan (see "How to Ask for an Alternative Work Option," page 130). "We like to think that two brains, two imaginations, two sets of creative ideas, two perspectives, are better than one," says Kost. "Plus, being in the office only two or three days a week keeps us from feeling burned out. We're also accountable to each other, as well as our boss and coworkers. That keeps us on our toes."

4. **Be flexible.** In most companies, a job share is still considered a gamble, so in return for the opportunity to prove that your plan can work, you need to be willing to make changes and concessions. For example, Kost and O'Neill agree to work an extra day or two occasionally if they're needed for an event or a major project. They also contribute "transition time" on their days off. When Kost comes in on Monday morning, she spends an hour on the phone with O'Neill reviewing their ongoing projects.
5. **Be ultra-organized.** Partners need to keep each other in the loop at all times. "Kathleen and I have a three- to four-page ongoing to-do list covering every project we're doing. We add details for each other all the time and note conversations with clients as well as any potential red flags. We *never* want someone to have to repeat something to me that they've already told Kathleen, or vice versa," says Kost. "Clients, coworkers, and our bosses must feel comfortable that we are one 'ear' and one voice."

After a year, Kost and O'Neill are thrilled with their job-share team. "It allows me to continue pursuing my career, *and* spend lots of time with my little girls, Samantha and Zoe, *and* keep my family organized (I'd hate to have to waste a lot of weekend family time with my husband and kids doing errands; instead, I can take care of these things

RESTRUCTURING YOUR JOB: ALTERNATIVE WORK SCHEDULES

Flexible work option	**What it is/how it works***	**Good news/ bad news**	**Benefits to your company**
Flextime	Employees vary their arrival and departure times from the standard *hours,* while still working a standard *length* day. A typical schedule might be 7:30 A.M. to 3:30 P.M.	*The good news:* • Traveling during off-peak hours may reduce commuting time. • You may require fewer hours of child care. • You may accomplish more at work if you're there during quiet times and are interrupted less often. • All of the above may reduce stress. *The bad news:* Coworkers may resent you for leaving "early" or coming in "late" (see "Beat the Clock-Watchers" on page 119 for tips on how to deal with this).	• With less stress and fewer interruptions, employees will be happier and more productive. • Office hours can be extended without adding extra personnel. • Turnover and absenteeism costs go down. • Useful recruiting tool.
Telecommuting	Employees meet full-time job responsibilities at a location other than the regular office (usually the employee's home).	*The good news:* • You eliminate commuting time and cost on days you telecommute. • You may require fewer hours of child care. • You may accomplish more at home since you'll be interrupted less often. • You'll have more flexibility	• With less stress and fewer interruptions, employees will be happier and more productive. • Absenteeism will be reduced because employees won't miss work due to child-care emergencies or kids' events.

RESTRUCTURING YOUR JOB: ALTERNATIVE WORK SCHEDULES (cont'd)

Flexible work option	What it is/how it works*	Good news/ bad news	Benefits to your company
Telecommuting (cont'd)		to schedule appointments and attend children's events during the day. • You'll be available in case of a child's illness or a child-care breakdown. • All of the above may reduce stress. *The bad news:* • Your career may suffer if your company culture rewards "face time" (see "Beat the Clock-Watchers" on page 119). • You may have to purchase your own computer or other equipment for your home office.	• Turnover costs will also be reduced—happy employees are less likely to leave their jobs. Also helps for recruiting. • Having several telecommuting employees may enable companies to save on real-estate costs. • Telecommuters help employers comply with environmental laws requiring them to help reduce pollution caused by commuting.
Compressed Workweek	Employees work a standard workweek compressed into fewer than five full working days.	*The good news:* • You'll have a day off each week or every other week—without losing pay. • You may travel during offpeak hours, thereby reducing commuting time. *The bad news:* • Your days in the office will be very	• Employees will complete a full-time job, but enjoy the lowered stress and increased productivity that come with reduced hours. • Companies may save on reduced turnover and absenteeism costs, plus gain an

RESTRUCTURING YOUR JOB: ALTERNATIVE WORK SCHEDULES (cont'd)

Flexible work option	What it is/how it works*	Good news/ bad news	Benefits to your company
		long, which could be draining.	important recruiting tool.
Part-Time	Employees work less than forty hours per week on a regular basis, with their salaries and benefits prorated. The reduction in hours may vary from 5 to 50 percent, and hours can be clustered in a few days or spread over the workweek.	*The good news:* • You'll enjoy more time with your kids. • You'll still earn money and keep current with your career. *The bad news:* • You'll earn less money. • You may land on the mommy track, perceived as less serious about your career because you've reduced your hours. • You may be asked to do more work than you can reasonably accomplish in your part-time schedule.	• Companies can retain a dedicated, happy, productive employee at a lower cost. • Over half of part-timers report *higher* productivity once they go part-time; their supervisor, clients, and colleagues agree, according to a Catalyst study. • Companies may save on reduced turnover and absenteeism costs, plus gain an important recruiting tool.
Job Sharing	Two employees divide the responsibilities of a full-time position.	*The good news:* • You'll enjoy more time with your kids. • You'll still earn money and keep current with your career. • You won't suffer from part-time "creep"—a part-time job can be stressful if it really can't be done in the time allotted.	• Employees will have less stress and enjoy their preferred work/ family balance, making them more productive. • Two heads are better than one. • Position is always covered: employees work part-time, but company gets

RESTRUCTURING YOUR JOB: ALTERNATIVE WORK SCHEDULES (cont'd)

Flexible work option	What it is/how it works*	Good news/ bad news	Benefits to your company
Job Sharing (cont'd)		Your partner will help you share the load. *The bad news:* • You'll earn less money. • You may land on the mommy track, perceived as less serious about your career because you've reduced your hours. • Your success depends in part on the competence and dedication of your partner (so choose wisely).	full-time work accomplished. • Partners can cover for each other in emergencies, reducing absenteeism. • Companies may save on reduced turnover costs, plus gain an important recruiting tool.

**Source:* WFD Consulting, Boston, Massachusetts.

midweek)," says Kost. "With my current schedule, there is little of the stress so often associated with balancing work and family."

How to Ask for an Alternative Work Option

1. Ask yourself what work/family problem you are trying to solve. Do you simply want more time at home? Are you seeking to reduce time spent commuting? Do you want to reduce your child-care costs? How might an alternative work option help?
2. Determine your employer's formal policies. Check your employee handbook or ask the human resources department. The company may already have a helpful program in place.

3. If no program is in place, develop a *written proposal* to present to your supervisor. You need to convince her (and perhaps her bosses, too) that this arrangement will benefit everyone. Include the following information in your proposal:
   - **Benefits to the company.** Don't focus on why *you* need this arrangement. Talk about how it will help your company. For example, if you work off hours or from home, you may be more productive because you'll deal with fewer distractions. It's important to anticipate any concerns your employers might have and address them in advance.
   - **Details on scheduling and availability.** Exactly what hours and days will you be in the office? How can you be reached during your time off? What equipment will you need at home? Will you need to shift any duties to a coworker or assistant?
   - **An evaluation plan.** Ask to use the alternative work option for a trial period of one to three months, with regularly scheduled check-in meetings with your supervisor. If she raises any concerns, you can work together to correct them—without losing your alternative work option.

Reinventing the Workplace

The number of women and mothers in the workplace is ever-increasing: 25,647,000 moms were in the labor force in 1998, up from 14,467,000 in 1975. That means the world of work is slowly becoming a friendlier place for parents. Mother after mother is proving that she can bring home the bacon and fry it up in a pan, although she might not use her grandmother's recipe (and her husband or child might wash the pan when she's done with it). As she shows that she's an efficient, productive worker *and* a good mom, she's paving the way for her daughter to do the same—with more support from her employers and the society she lives in.

PART FOUR

PERSONAL TIME

How to Find Time for Yourself Without Feeling Guilty

How many of you turned to this section first? In a recent survey, 86 percent of *Working Mother* readers said they "always" or "frequently" give up personal time when they're in a time crunch—and that implies that they have some personal time in the first place. The survey revealed that only around one third of moms make time for themselves more than once a week; 21 percent make time for themselves only every few months or less; and 7 percent never make time for themselves at all.

Many working mothers do a good job of managing their work time and keeping things organized at home (they have to, or they'd never be home for dinner and no one in the family would ever have clean underwear). But clearly the one thing that eludes them is time for themselves—to reconnect with their spouse, see friends, exercise, pursue a hobby, volunteer in the community, or simply relax, blissfully alone.

The truth is, spending time on yourself and on activities you enjoy is critical to keeping your life in balance, your stress level low, and the rest of your family happy. You can't take care of them well—or, more important, enjoy your time with them—if you are burnt out and resentful because your own needs aren't being met. Whether it's a reluctance to put yourself first—even for a few hours a week—or an inability to find the time to do it that gets in the way, the strategies in this section will help you claim those precious, revitalizing hours.

- **They Say It's Like Riding a Bicycle** (Chapter 15) focuses on techniques to maintain or rediscover intimacy and connection with your partner even with a too-crowded schedule.
- **Let's Be Friends** (Chapter 16) addresses the enormously important issue of friendships—a vital network of support and nurturing that working moms often find hard to maintain.
- **Time Off** (Chapter 17) looks at the rare and precious moments you find to spend alone—and suggests ways to make time for this ultimate, revitalizing pleasure.

- **Fitting in Fitness** (Chapter 18) aims to help you find the time, energy, and inclination to exercise regularly. After all, it is one of the best cures for stress, depression, frustration, and lethargy ever invented.
- **"Right! And in My Spare Time I Garden"** (Chapter 19) outlines ways to make time for hobbies and favorite activities.
- **Being Part of Your Community** (Chapter 20) examines the importance of finding time to volunteer in community-based activities.

| 15 |

They Say It's Like Riding a Bicycle

Relationship experts and real moms agree: To keep marriages strong, husbands and wives need private time together. As much as they love their children, moms and dads must find ways to concentrate on each other without the kids around.

Sex therapist Lonnie Barbach, Ph.D., compares marriage to a business, to which you must devote time not only at its inception, but always. "Years after you marry, you have to keep going out on dates, telling him he looks great, and so forth. You need to do the things you did when the relationship was new, except now you may have to make a more conscious effort to do them," she says.

Readers agree that nurturing their marriage is an important foundation for their family. "One-on-one time is very important to the marital relationship; without it, there is no family. To keep both healthy, there has to be a delicate balance," says one mom, a computer programmer with three young children.

California mom Donna Beveridge says she considers relationship time an investment in the future. "Things change as kids grow. When our boys were young we had less time and more 'rush hours.' But as they grow, remember to spend time with your partner—before long it's just the two of you and you need to keep in touch," says Beveridge, a child-care coordinator whose sons are now twelve and twenty-two.

Let's Talk About Sex

"**S**ex and the working mom" doesn't quite evoke the same passionate image as "sex and the single girl." With sleep a rare and precious commodity, sex can easily become the last thing on your mind. Only 16 percent of mothers answering our recent time-management survey said they have as much time as they would like for lovemaking. And that's a shame, because besides being a key element of your relationship with your partner, and a lot of fun, sex is good for your health!

Women who have sex at least once a week produce higher levels of estrogen. That hormonal boost keeps your bones strong and healthy, improves cardiovascular health, and might even help ward off depression, according to research at the Athena Institute in Chester Springs, Pennsylvania. Even a good snuggle works. "With any kind of intimate touch, levels of oxytocin, the chemical that makes you feel calm and decreases blood pressure levels, go higher," says Helen Fisher, Ph.D., an anthropologist and the author of *Anatomy of Love.* Oxytocin is also the "bonding" chemical that makes us feel attached to one another. It is stimulated (much more in women than men) by intimate touching, affection, and physical contact and may explain why women associate love and sex more closely than men do.

To keep your sex life on track, even when daily pressures keep you hopping from dawn till dusk:

- **Broaden your definition of sex.** "I encourage couples not to view sex as a step-by-step process with only one goal in mind—intercourse," says Chicago sex therapist Jennifer Knopf, Ph.D. "I ask couples to view sex in an unstructured way, one in which they'll be open to experimenting with whatever makes them feel good at the moment."

- **Be open to physical pleasure,** even if you feel you're too tired or "not in the mood." "Sometimes I start out thinking I definitely don't want sex. But pretty often I find out I wasn't as tired as I thought I was," says one mom, a psychologist with a four-year-old son.
- **Keep things in perspective.** Don't use your sex life as the only arbiter of how strong your marriage is. "Passion is often linked to a stage of family development," says Knopf. Understandably, many couples go through a sexual low patch just after they have a baby or when they have several very young children. "I wouldn't be too worried at this stage if your sex life is less than stellar."

Date Night

One of the best aphrodisiacs, says Jennifer Knopf, is a standing Saturday night date. A special date-night ritual helps you keep your commitment to connection with your partner. You both acknowledge that you're making an effort to keep your relationship vital. The time is especially set aside for you, and you can look forward to time together on a regular basis. If you make the effort, you'll probably discover what moms told us in a recent survey: The key to finding time for making love is getting organized. Among the mothers that *Working Mother* surveyed, more than half who said they had enough time for lovemaking also said they are good time-managers.

Your kids also benefit from your regular date night. "My husband and I love our children, and we show it and tell them at every opportunity. But our children also know that moms and dads need 'couple time' together. They don't love it when we go out, but we explain that's what keeps us happy as a couple and connected as a family," says mother of three Betsy Kapulskey, a writer and public relations specialist from New Jersey. Knopf agrees. "Children need to see a happy marriage between their parents," she says. When parents are close, kids feel secure, and they're seeing a healthy example they'll take with them into adulthood.

At first, it will take some effort to come up with things to do and to arrange for child care, but practice makes perfect. You'll soon develop a roster of baby-sitters you can trust and a repertoire of activities you enjoy. Ideas for finding both follow.

Finding a Baby-Sitter

Your date night won't go far without a caregiver for your kids, and you won't enjoy yourself unless that caregiver is reliable and trustworthy. So child care is a priority.

Where to find a good sitter:

- Enlist **family members.** If grandparents are near, you may have it made. Most enjoy spending some one-on-one time with their grandkids, so it's a win-win situation. Another resource: siblings with young children of their own. One mother of two kids, ages four and seven, swaps baby-sitting time with her sister, who has a two-year-old. Each family provides care for the other once a month. "This way we each get to have one date a month, we know that our children are well cared for, and we get the benefit of spending time with our niece," she explains.
- Make a similar arrangement with a **friend or neighbor.**
- Formalize the deal with a **baby-sitting co-op,** in which you join with a group of families to provide care for each other's kids. Start by enlisting a group of nearby families, setting general policies

WORKING MOM'S WORDS OF WISDOM

"Leave Home for Good Conversation"

My husband and I talk most effectively and most connectedly when we're not in our house. It seems that the neutral spaces—restaurants or movie theaters—bring on meaningful conversations.

—**Jeanmarie Nielsen,** *college professor and mother of two kids, ages seven and eight* (how much notice is required for cancellation, for example) and establishing a payment system—some groups use scrip or simply track and trade hours. When you're ready to go out, all you need to do is consult the list of member families to find someone who can care for your children. Then you return the favor another time.

- Recruit a responsible **high school or college student** (or better yet, several). Ask friends, relatives, and teachers for recommendations, or post signs in the education department at a local college. Be sure to ask for references and spend time with the caregiver before leaving her alone with your kids. Sign your favorite caregiver up for a standing engagement—every Saturday, for example, or every other Friday. You could even split the task between two caregivers. This will save you the chore of lining up a sitter every time you go out. Alternatively, work your schedule around theirs. "Instead of planning a date and then looking for sitters, I call all our sitters and ask them for free times and then plan our dates times accordingly," says Wendy Ann Postlethwaite, a Massachusetts marketing consultant and mother of three daughters, ages eight, ten, and twelve.
- Find out if your **child-care center** has extended-care nights. Some centers stay open until 10 or 11 P.M. one Friday per month, for an extra charge, so parents can have an evening out. Another option: See if any of the teachers in the center would be willing to baby-sit occasionally. Many will welcome the chance to earn a little extra money.

Safety Checklist

Be sure to leave your baby-sitter the following information (visit the American Red Cross's Web site for a list you can download and print: www.redcross.org/hss):

- Where you'll be
- Cellular phone number

- Local emergency number
- Doctor's name and number
- Poison control center number
- Neighbor's name and number
- Hospital name
- Medical insurance information
- Important medical information, such as allergies
- Instructions and dosages of any medications your children are taking
- Your expected return time
- Your home phone number and address
- Name of nearest cross street
- Children's names and ages

Keeping a Baby-Sitter

To keep your caregivers happy, be upfront—and sensible—about your needs and expectations. While it's not unreasonable to ask your sitter to pick up the playroom after the kids go to sleep, it usually isn't a good idea to require that she scrub down the kitchen or throw in a load of laundry. She's there to play with the kids and keep them safe.

Make sure your caregivers know exactly what kids expect and how to discipline them if there's any trouble. You should go over your bedtime routine, for example, and give your baby-sitter a few ideas for what to do if kids balk at turning off the television or brushing their teeth. It's tough for a sitter when children argue, "But Mommy lets me!" Give her as much ammunition as you can from the beginning so she can say, "Nope, Mom says no TV after eight o'clock. Let's go read a story."

Your caregiver will also appreciate it if you:

- Keep your word about when you'll be home, and call if you're unavoidably late.
- Make sure you have a variety of snacks available, especially if you'll be gone for several hours.
- Pay her promptly and generously (check in with other moms in

your neighborhood or at your child-care center to find out the going rate).

Kids' Night In

Suggest these activities to your children's caregiver . . . and brainstorm with her to come up with more ideas.

- A special "baby-sitter box" filled with toys that are used only when a caregiver comes over.
- A craft project: With your kids, flip through a few craft books and choose an activity they can do with their caregiver (do this in advance in case you need to set aside any supplies).
- Cooking—especially a sweet treat like cookies or Rice Krispie treats.
- A rental movie or video/computer game (particularly good if this is a rare treat).
- Board games and puzzles.
- A special book, particularly a longer one, that the caregiver reads whenever she's there—the kids will look forward to story time.
- With a regular baby-sitter, start a picture book. Each time the caregiver comes over, everyone can draw pictures. After you have a bunch stockpiled, make holes with a three-hole punch and place in a binder, or simply tie pages together with string. Kids can keep adding to it, even making chapters: one with special birthday cards for mom, one with spooky Halloween characters, one for Chanukah, and so on.
- Slumber party: Turn off the lights and tell stories, or use a flashlight to draw letters and numbers on the ceiling and have kids guess what they are.

Beyond Dinner and a Movie

Now that you've gotten the kids taken care of, you need to figure out what you're going to do on your date! Your date-planning skills may have gotten a little rusty over the years, so here's a guide to dates beyond dinner and a movie.

If you share an interest in an activity or sport, you've got lots of ready-made ideas. Also, scan your area's newspapers and magazines for listings of movies, performances, and exhibits you might both be interested in. If you have a favorite museum, concert venue, or sports team, treat yourself to a membership, concert series, or season tickets. Advantages: You'll save money; you'll receive information on special members-only events; you'll be motivated to get the most out of the money you've spent by sticking to your plans.

If you don't share a hobby or favorite activity, try something new together: Take dancing lessons, join a gourmet cooking club, take a wine-tasting class, learn how to scuba dive. See what your community center or local college has to offer. Browse together at a bookstore or music store.

To keep each other guessing, try taking turns planning "blind" date nights. Each time, one of you has full license to take the other person wherever you wish—and keep it a surprise until you get there. Not only does this add an element of surprise to the date, but you may be exposed to things you may otherwise not choose to do (and have fun doing them!).

Keep the Connection

Dedicated date nights aren't the only way to stay in close touch with your spouse. You can and should look for other opportunities to reconnect, say the experts. "Of course, bringing home a bunch of flowers or buying your husband's favorite dessert now and then is great. But married partners should try to keep a steady stream of signals of acceptance going between them—a kiss for no reason, a smile for no reason, a little comment that shows you like what the other said or did," says Evelyn Streit Cohen, M.S., M.A., a marriage and family therapist in New York City.

Try a daily thirty-second hug (it feels longer than it sounds), says Cohen. Just before you leave in the morning, or when you first see each other in the evening, is a good time. "Everyone, including your spouse, responds to genuine praise, thanks, and simple, heartfelt compliments on a regular basis. Try to give your partner this gift every day," says John Gottman, Ph.D., who's done pioneering research on why marriages succeed.

Opportunities for meaningful moments abound if you look for them carefully—and make a commitment to using them wisely. "We've started a walking program, so we get about thirty minutes of time together after dinner," says mother of two Trish Elker. "We do our walks four or five times a week, and they've been great. The children are old enough (they're nine and twelve) to be left alone for that time, and we sometimes carry a cell phone if they need us. Until we started walking, we never had enough time together," says Elker, a transcriptionist who lives in Pennsylvania.

Take full advantage of the post-bedtime hours. "Our haven time is when the children are in bed," says Nebraska mom Jeanmarie Nielsen. "Sometimes we talk, sometimes we don't, but we're in the same room together, both doing what we enjoy (he is a computer geek and I quilt)."

Diane Ginther, a human resources manager from Kansas, also treasures these evening hours. She advises other moms to "set an early bedtime for the kids and stick with it. When they get too old to go to sleep that early, enforce a prebedtime time in their rooms, so that they are reading, studying, or playing quietly on their own for that time period when they used to be in bed. That way you maintain that private time you got used to when they were little. Since our kids have always had to get up early for day care, it has been easier to get them to bed early."

Similarly, Cinta Burgos and her husband plan romantic dinner-and-a-movie evenings in their home after their four-year-old goes to bed. "It works well to give us time with each other, yet we can stop the movie if we get tired or something comes up with our son," says Burgos, an engineer from Massachusetts.

For daytime connections:

- Make a lunch date. It's a great jumpstart to your afternoon, and you don't need special child-care arrangements.
- Tele-connect. "We talk to each other over the phone when things are so hectic we can't have time together any other way," says Liz Moore, a legal clerk from Nevada with three daughters, ages ten, twelve, and fifteen. Other moms use E-mail and pagers to send messages and love notes to their partners (for privacy, most develop a secret code).
- Master the ability to adapt. "We've learned to have meaningful conversations with chaos in the next room," says Ann Withington, an administrative assistant from Maine with two children, ages nine and twelve.

Weathering a Conversational Dry Spell

So you've found the baby-sitter, picked a restaurant, and settled in for a lovely evening with your mate. Now what? Can you talk about anything but Josh's runny nose or Caitlin's potty-training progress? Try these tactics:

- **Pay attention to each other's passions.** "Find out more about what your spouse finds interesting, even if it's not the number one priority in your life," says Susan RoAne, a communications expert and author of *What Do I Say Next?*
- **Don't discount the current-events option.** As long as you're respectful, it doesn't matter whether you agree or not. You'll listen to your neighbors' opinions—even a stranger you see on TV—about the latest news. Why not find out what your partner's views are?
- **Dream about the future together.** Play the "if we won the lottery" game or ask your husband what his fantasy job is. Reminiscing about the past works, too.
- **Know what's going on in his life.** What's he working on right now? Did he have a big meeting scheduled for today? "This way

you can be more specific than 'How was your day?' " RoAne says. "If you share something that happened to you, you can encourage a dialogue by asking for his feedback."

- **Look on the bright side.** "Begin discussions in an upbeat way—acknowledge something good," RoAne says. Notice what's going well in your life and your family and talk about it.

16

Let's Be Friends

Even for busy working moms with precious time to spare, friends are an important part of the web that makes life enjoyable—even, sometimes, merely manageable. They not only enrich your life; they may lengthen it, too. Women who don't have a support network—an active group of friends, relatives, and neighbors to rely on—are more susceptible to both illness and depression than those who do have such a group. That's according to research by Nancy Marshall, Ed.D., senior research scientist at the Center for Research on Women at Wellesley College.

Friends can save you in sticky situations—when you need child care at the last minute, just had a huge fight with your mother, or can't find a good recipe for cupcakes (and the class party is tomorrow). To make sure you'll have such a circle of friends in your time of need, you need to cultivate it now.

Meet and Greet

Many women find that once they have children, their friendships change dramatically. Pals you were previously close to sometimes can't relate to your fascination with toilet training, your love of Sesame Street, or your child-care woes. Worse yet, they may find it hard to understand why you don't have as much time for them as you once did. Even when you're both moms, if one of you is employed and the other is a stay-at-home mom, the gap in your circumstances can be tough to bridge.

If you feel you're lacking in the friend department, try tapping these resources.

- **The parents of your children's friends** are a popular place to start. Many families develop a lasting bond when their kids attend the same child-care center. You're likely to have much in common, and you see each other regularly at drop-off and pickup time, birthday parties, and play dates.
- **Neighbors** share a common interest in creating a sense of community and keeping their street clean and inviting. To reach out to them, consider joining a block association or neighborhood watch program.
- **Online communities** for moms are blossoming all over cyberspace. *Working Mother* has a Web site (www.workingmother.com) featuring resources, articles, and ideas, plus message boards and live chats. The Cybermom Dot Com (www.thecybermom.com) provides visitors with information and chats on all things related to families. For friends who come right into your virtual mailbox, there are listserves such as NetWorkingMoms (for information, visit www.networkingmoms.com or call 1-888-492-6832) and WMOMS (to subscribe, send the message "subscribe <your e-mail address> wmoms" to majordomo@world.std.com).
- Join a **church, gym, volunteer organization, or special interest club** (see Chapter 20 for more tips).

Find Time for Friends

Use some of the tricks you've no doubt already learned as a working mom to make room for friends in your busy life: Prioritize, schedule, and multitask. Prioritizing can mean not just making an effort to keep friends in your life, but also to keep only those who really enrich your days. If you pare back to just those friends whom you truly enjoy, you'll have more time for them and you'll feel better about spending it.

Scheduling time with your friends is often a must. Most of your friends are like you—they have busy lives, ruled by the to-do list and the calendar. If you wait until the last minute to make plans, chances are you won't. It may be discouraging to have to wait several weeks until you find a time when you're both available, but getting a date on the calendar keeps you from letting that moment slip away.

You might have to get creative in order to make time for your friends. "When I take a day off from work it is usually because my kids are off from school and I end up planning some outing with them," says New Jersey mother of two Elizabeth Verri. "I am seriously considering getting my friend to take a day off to just go out together. We try to meet periodically for dinner, but it ends up being a late night during the week," says Verri, who is a vice president at a stock brokerage.

As for multitasking: Consider ways to combine a social visit with something else you want to make time for.

- Enlist a friend to accompany you on your Saturday morning errands; chances are she needs to go the supermarket and the discount store, too, and you can top off the morning with a lunch out, matinee, or manicure.
- Make a friend who shares your hobby or learn something new with an old friend.
- Sign up your pal to be your exercise buddy. One pair of New York City moms jogs together in Central Park nearly every Saturday and Sunday morning. "We have the best conversations during our runs," says one. "We can cover so much more than we would in a phone call: On the first day we'll talk all about work, then on the second day we move on to our kids and husbands!"

- Catch up by chatting on a cordless phone while you fold laundry or do other small household chores.
- Invite a friend over to help you bake cookies or cupcakes for your child's birthday; she can help out and you can spend time together at the same time. For the holiday season, expand this idea to a cookie exchange: Invite several friends over (about five, advises *Working Mother* food editor Susan Lilly Ott) and ask each person to bring a batch of her favorite holiday treats—one dozen for each family in the exchange, preplated and divided—and copies of its recipe. Then each family will take home an assortment of goodies.

17

Time Off

True time off—those precious hours and minutes when you have no responsibilities to anyone or anything, large or small—is the Shangri-la of working motherhood. "Asking what I would do if I had more time to myself is like asking, 'If you won the lottery, what would you do?' " says Ilyssa Esgar-DeCasperis, a New York lawyer and consumer advocate with two sons, ages one and five. Most moms would agree; time alone can seem like the most precious—and most unlikely—gift they could ever dream of receiving.

A full 70 percent of the two hundred–plus moms questioned in a *Working Mother* survey said they don't have enough time alone. Of those, about half say they resent not having enough time; the rest say they understand it or are resigned to it: "I knew the rules when I signed up," says Racine Tucker-Hamilton, a journalist from Maryland and mother of two young boys.

The biggest obstacle to finding time for yourself may be your own guilt. "Moving to the 'I'm worth it' position is a long-term struggle for most women," says therapist and author Jo Ann Larsen. It's partly because moms are busy and tired, says Larsen, but it's also because they feel they don't deserve any time they take for themselves. What they should know, she says, is that "investing in yourself doesn't mean that you give more to yourself than to someone else. It simply means that you give as much, that you acknowledge that you count and that you take responsibility for growing up and out as a human being."

One mom gets around this by taking care of must-do's along with want-to's. "I feel guilty spending time on myself. So I plan a 'Mommy's Day Off' once every six months. I take a day off from work, but leave my son in day care. I spend the entire day on myself. I usually schedule essential appointments, like dental visits, for the early morning, so that I don't feel as guilty about spending a full eight hours on myself," says Michelle Schmitz, who lives in Virginia with her husband and two-year-old son. "Then I take myself someplace nice for lunch and spend the afternoon shopping, or at the movies, or getting a haircut. I usually feel very refreshed after my day off and it makes it much easier to give one hundred percent of my time to other people during the rest of the year," says Schmitz, who works for the federal government as a special agent. "I'd love to do this more often—if I had more vacation days!"

Being alone is clearly important. Spending time on yourself—whether it's reading a grown-up novel instead of *Goodnight Moon* or listening to Beethoven instead of Barney—rejuvenates and refreshes like nothing else. So how can you make it happen? In this chapter we'll discuss how to find this time—and hoard it.

How I Spend My Down Time

From a *Working Mother* survey of more than two hundred reader panelists.

- Read/watch TV/other entertainment: 56 percent
- Exercise: 36 percent

- Socialize with friends: 30 percent
- Hobbies: 23 percent
- Volunteer work: 21 percent
- Relax and do nothing: 20 percent

WORKING MOM'S WORDS OF WISDOM

"Adopt an Attitude!"

These moms have moved beyond guilt and feel great about it:

- I used to feel guilty about spending time alone, but now I know I deserve it, I need it, and I have to have it to be at my best for my family.

  —**Toni Thompson,** *pediatric occupational therapist and single mom of two*

- Why should I feel guilty about spending time on myself? I'm a person too!

  —**Donna Beveridge,** *married, child care coordinator, and mother of two*

- I absolutely don't feel guilty about spending time on myself. Being emotionally healthy is very important. I have people counting on me—at home and at work.

  —**Michele Armstrong,** *married, emergency communications operator, and mother of one*

Make Time Work for You

Time-use experts John Robinson and Geoffrey Godbey say working moms have thirty whole hours of *free* time every single week! Laying claim to those thirty hours isn't easy, but it can be done. First, you need to become more conscious of your time—sensitive to those bits and pieces you have. Next, you'll need to take a stand and make some hard choices about how you spend your time. Finally, take control by arranging the tasks you want to do and those you need to do to your best advantage.

Become Conscious of Your Time

The best way to do this, says Robinson, is to keep a time diary. For a week, note what you are doing every minute and how long it takes you (see chart on page 155). Then add it up at the end of the week, breaking down what you've done into categories. Robinson uses the following: paid work, household work, child care, shopping, personal needs (eating, sleeping, grooming), and free time.

Sample Time Diary Entries

Note what you do with free hours (okay, free minutes): Flop in front of the TV? Curl up with a book? Grab a cup of coffee with a friend? Also look at how they are concentrated. Perhaps you didn't realize that Tuesday evenings are pretty open because your husband and daughter play softball together that night, or that your baby has been falling asleep earlier these days. "Things look different when you've actually written down where your time goes," says Robinson.

Make Choices

Now examine your time diary again, studying the time that's *not* free. What activities are you doing that you don't enjoy? Can you stop? You may not like attending PTA meetings, for example, because they're held

Tuesday

TIME	ACTIVITY	TIME SPENT	CATEGORY
6:15–6:30	Get up; have cup of coffee alone	15 minutes	Free time
6:30–6:40	Shower, comb hair	10 minutes	Personal needs
6:40–6:50	Put on makeup	10 minutes	Personal needs
6:50–7:00	Wake kids; start them dressing	10 minutes	Child care
7:00–7:10	Dress myself	10 minutes	Personal needs
7:10–7:15	Help kids finish and get downstairs	5 minutes	Child care
2:00–2:20	Conference call with sales staff	20 minutes	Paid work
2:20–2:30	Call sister to confirm weekend plans	10 minutes	Free time
2:30–3:10	Meet with designer to go over new brochure	40 minutes	Paid work
5:45–6:20	Prepare dinner (while reciting spelling words with son)	35 minutes	Household work, child care
6:20–6:45	Eat dinner	25 minutes	Personal needs
6:45–7:00	Supervise kitchen cleanup while preparing tomorrow's lunches	15 minutes	Household work, child care
7:00–7:30	Watch video with kids	30 minutes	Free time

in the evening and tend to drag on. Perhaps you'd be better off taking an occasional vacation day to chaperone a field trip. You're still involved with your child's schooling, but you've traded an unpleasant, time-sucking activity for a more fulfilling one. Or say you're snapping at your kids, feeling run-down and tired because you don't get enough exercise. You may find that you're happiest—and can be a better mom—if you resign your post as Brownie troop leader and take up volleyball instead. Or perhaps you have a weekly staff meeting at 8 A.M. that causes you to rush through your morning routine. Can you suggest to your boss that the meeting be moved to 8:30? Some of your coworkers might be wishing for the same change.

Other chores and duties can't be avoided, but they can be arranged to fit your schedule. You may "buy" weekend time by accomplishing weekly errands, such as grocery shopping, during the week—perhaps during your lunch break or in the evenings after your children have gone to bed. Or you may have more time for exercise, for example, if you do it as soon as you wake up in the morning so that there's less chance something will come up to distract you.

One mom found that eliminating exercise from her day didn't help her manage her time after all. "Some time ago, I tried to eliminate horseback riding in order to put more time into home, career, and family. However, it wasn't long before I missed the horses to no end. It was as though I was missing my soul," she says. "So now, three or four mornings a week, I get up at about 6:30, ride, finish my barn chores about 7:30, take a quick shower, and drive the children to school. Then I head to the office refreshed and ready to go."

Take Control

Research by Rosalind Barnett, a senior scholar at the Murray Research Center at Radcliffe College in Boston and coauthor of *She Works/He Works: How Two-Income Families Are Happier, Healthier, and Better Off,* indicates that what's really important is not so much what we do, but whether we feel in control of it.

There are several strategies you can use to take more control of your time and your tasks:

- **Redistribute tasks.** Pack weekdays full to have weekends off, if that's what suits you. Alternatively, relax during your lunch hour and evenings, but dedicate a few hours on Saturday or Sunday morning to errands.

WORKING MOM'S WORDS OF WISDOM

"Find Ways to Fit In What Matters"

About a year ago, I really thought about what I could do more of if I didn't work (i.e., what was missing). Two things I really wanted to do were exercise and read. So, I began to make these more of a priority and worked them into my schedule. I am much happier about it.

To fit in more reading, I have learned to make going to the library a semimonthly occurrence. Because the books become due in two weeks' time, I am basically compelled to go to the library frequently. I read on vacation when we take long car trips and on my commute. I've even met some fellow commuters with whom I exchange books and we've become friends.

For exercise: We purchased a treadmill for our house about a year ago. I try to go on it at least three times a week—at night, after the day's work is done.

—**Elizabeth Verri,** *married, vice president of a stock brokerage, and mother of two*

- **Be realistic.** If you try to overcram the free minutes you do come across, they won't be very pleasant. Instead of trying to clean the whole kitchen in the five minutes before you have to leave for work, just make sure the dishes are loaded in the dishwasher. Or leave them for later and choose to spend that five minutes sipping your coffee, so you'll be refreshed and ready to hit the road.
- **Advance your goals.** Do you want to exercise more, find more time for friends, read to your children more? When you have a little chunk of time—much more common than a sudden discovery of a free afternoon—use it for something meaningful. In just ten to twenty minutes, you can take a short walk, make a phone call, or cuddle up with the kids and a storybook.
- **Break down tasks** into smaller pieces. If you're faced with finding a new child-care provider or cleaning the basement, resolve to

make one phone call or clean out one box every day for a week. You'll be able to carve out those fifteen minutes a day much more easily than several hours all together, and the task won't seem so onerous.

- **Say no.** This is often a hard one to face for eager-to-please women. It takes practice and a good deal of self-discipline. Remind yourself: "If you want to please everyone, you'll never have any free time," says time researcher Geoffrey Godbey.

WORKING MOM'S WORDS OF WISDOM

"Be the Center of Your Attention"

I try to make time for myself. It could be just fifteen minutes at the end of the day to have a warm cup of liquid and sit in the quiet of my home with candlelight. I believe it's important to reserve time for yourself so that you do not lose yourself in all the running around of the day and meeting schedules, whether they are yours or others'. We give so much time to others that we need to reserve some time for ourselves. These few minutes of time alone helps me to center again and not feel that I am cheated by the hustle and bustle of some days.

—**Sue Toy,** *research analyst and single mother of an eight-year-old boy*

18

Fitting in Fitness

You know it's good for you. You know it will help you feel better, stay in shape, and live longer. You'd be happy to exercise—if only you could find the time.

Trust us: You can. We have lots of ideas for how—and why—to make fitness an integral part of your daily routine. Your first step, of course, is to get motivated to make exercise a priority.

Instead of thinking of exercise as another thing to squeeze in, consider this: Exercise actually *creates* energy, says Wayne Wescott, Ph.D., an exercise consultant to the YMCA. Far from sapping your strength, it keeps your body raring to go—and then come nightfall, relaxes you so you'll sleep more soundly.

WORKING MOM'S WORDS OF WISDOM

"You Have to Expend Energy to Gain Energy"

After the birth of my twins, I just ran out of energy. Even though I was able to lose my pregnancy weight by dieting for a few months, I was constantly tired and getting sick. I knew I had to build up my strength.

So once the twins were sleeping through the night, I started using exercise videos to do fifteen minutes of calisthenics and thirty minutes of aerobics in the evening. I also got a double jogging stroller so that after my husband gets home from work, he can watch our older son while I take the twins for a forty-five-minute run.

I've been following this regimen three to six times a week for a year now, and I feel better and I look better. Best of all, I have so much more energy to take care of my boys. Exercising sure improved my life.

—**Betsy Spratt,** *mechanical engineer and mother of three boys under four*

Get Motivated

More than just finding time, making room for fitness can mean an attitude adjustment. You might need to play a few mind games with yourself. Don't be afraid to use every trick in the book to keep you motivated, especially at first. Eventually, you'll find a routine that works for you and exercise that you enjoy—and you'll be looking forward to that burst of energy you get from a good workout. Until that time, try these strategies to keep you inspired and encouraged:

- **Focus on the health benefits**—the list is long, including everything from weight loss to boosting immune strength, fighting heart disease, easing depression, and controlling PMS symptoms.
- **Set a goal** or set several: Your long-term goal might be to keep your heart and lungs healthy. Your short-term goal might be to get in shape for a charity walkathon, fit into a favorite pair of jeans that have become too snug, or simply to relieve stress.

- **Chart your improvements** (on paper is even better than just in your head). How many more sets of crunches or biceps curls can you do today, as opposed to last month? How far can you run in twenty minutes? What level do you set your exercise bike or stair-climber on?

  Focus on fitness achievements instead of pounds and inches, but do work toward a goal. If you'd like to build your endurance, then how far you can run in twenty minutes isn't as important as the fact that you could run two miles a day last month, and this month you're up to three miles a day.
- **Enlist a workout buddy.** It might be your husband, a good friend, even a coworker who makes sure you take a brisk walk together after lunch. Your commitment to your partner gives your exercise plan a little more importance than if you go it alone.

Strength in Numbers

More than 80 percent of the nearly one thousand readers who responded to a *Working Mother* survey work out from three to seven days a week. One third of those spend an hour or more exercising each time.

Still, almost 75 percent of them say that it is extremely or somewhat difficult to find the time: In a recent time-management study, 43 percent of moms said exercise is what they sacrifice when time is short.

How Much? And Why Bother?

If you're just beginning an exercise program or making a commitment to jump-start a languishing fitness routine, start slowly. Set a goal of exercising for just thirty minutes, two to three times a week, and then build up from there. Surely you can get up half an hour early, set aside your lunch break, or leave your husband in charge of the kids after dinner just two or three days out of seven. Once you've squeezed this in, you can work on increasing the time you dedicate to exercise.

The American Heart Association, the American College of Sports Medicine, and the Centers for Disease Control and Prevention all now recommend everyone do thirty minutes or more of moderately intense physical activity on most or, preferably, all days of the week. But keep in mind that new research has shown that breaking up those thirty minutes of exercise into smaller chunks of time is just as effective and beneficial as doing thirty minutes all at once. Daily activity can be divided up into as many as three ten-minute segments.

"Moderately intense exercise" can include sports such as aerobics, jogging, and cycling, or activities such as raking leaves, washing your car by hand, or playing a quick game of soccer with your kids. As for the health benefits: Exercise improves cardiovascular fitness and lowers blood pressure and cholesterol levels—which means it's good for your heart.

Becoming more fit can slow the hands of time, says Dr. Steven Blair, director of research and epidemiology at the Cooper Institute of Aerobics Research in Dallas. He points out that "unfit people start to develop physical limitations twenty to twenty-five years earlier than people who are more fit." He also cites evidence that exercise improves sleep, the ability to handle stress, the functioning of the immune system, and the mental outlook. People who exercise regularly feel better and have more energy, he says, which would also contribute to a better sex life.

Finding Time

Many moms discover that their best bet is to make exercise a part of their schedule by taking a class. "My ballet classes are scheduled and at night, when it's easy for my husband to do parent duty solo," says a Virginia mom with two preschoolers. If you've committed to—and paid for—ten weeks of swimming lessons or aerobics classes, it's tougher to wimp out and do something else with the time you've set aside for exercise.

Still, it's important to be flexible. After all, that's a working mom's middle name. Try these tactics:

- Use the gym, your home, and the outdoors.
- Make workouts interesting through variety. Sunday, take a bike ride with your family; Tuesday, go to an aerobics class at lunchtime; Thursday, wake up early and speed-walk before breakfast.
- Variety also cuts down on excuses: If the weather prohibits an outdoor walk or jog, switch to plan B (a swim at your health club) or plan C (an at-home workout with an exercise video or stationary bike).
- Don't obsess over time. Fifteen or thirty minutes is better than nothing, and your workouts add up over time. It's more important to do a little something than to skip a day; otherwise you'll relapse into a habit of not having enough time for exercise.
- Don't be rigid about scheduling either: If you normally exercise first thing in the morning, don't throw in the towel if a sick child or unusually early meeting gets in the way. Try to fit in a lunchtime or evening workout instead.
- Ask for help. "It's extremely helpful to have a husband who recognizes that exercise is necessary for my physical and emotional well-being," said a social worker and mother of four who responded to *Working Mother*'s fitness survey. "I have always talked to him about how important I believe exercise is for the whole family, and not only does he fill in with child care in the morning if I need to run, but he exercises regularly, too. And the kids also see that exercise isn't a sometime event, but a part of our daily lives."

As you develop an exercise habit, keep your expectations reasonable. Remember that celebrities and professional athletes have hours of time and a cast of thousands to keep them in the shape they're in—and they are paid millions of dollars to look that good. In essence, it is their job to have a perfect physique. If someone paid you that much you'd look that good, too. Trying to end up looking like Demi Moore will only lead to frustration—and probably injury.

19

"Right! And in My Spare Time, I Garden"

Research shows that the more diverse your life is, the healthier and happier you'll be. Psychologists at Yale University, for example, measured the complexity of people's interests and lives. Those with more complex lives were less likely to be depressed or suffer from bad moods, headaches, and other ailments.

Developing a personal interest can give you a booster shot of self-esteem. If you can see yourself in many roles (as a mom, a professional, a runner, a cook, a mystery lover), you'll better appreciate your many talents. This creates a psychological and physical buffer zone around you. "Whether you cultivate a garden or a new friendship, developing variety can make you healthier and less vulnerable to setbacks," say Robert Ornstein, Ph.D., and David Sobel, M.D., coauthors of *Healthy Pleasures.* "In trying times it is more likely you can find solace within. You can activate a different, separate area of your life that is satisfying, fulfilling, and the source of positive feelings."

Keeping up with a passion can even be a boon for your marriage and family: "Busy women have more realistic expectations of other family members," says St. Louis psychotherapist Doris Wild Helmering. "They tend to be less angry—which makes them easier to live with. They aren't relying on a husband to keep them entertained. And women with different interests bring more to the table. There's more to talk about and share, so the relationship becomes richer."

Getting into the Hobby Habit

The first step to finding time for your interests may be to give up guilt. "My advice to a woman who's feeling guilty about doing something on her own would be simply to go ahead and do it," says Helmering. If you do, you'll see results—a happier you means a happier family—and you'll forget about those guilty feelings.

Another way to get a grip on guilt and make room for your passions is to tell others, especially your family, how excited you are about what you're doing. They'll better understand why you aren't available to them during these times. And they'll become a cheering section, proud that you're learning to ski or fascinated by your newfound skill at oil painting.

If you need a jump start, look for fellow aficionados. Joining a book club, for example, may motivate you to make time for a novel every month or two. Signing up for a class or club—whether in person or online—can rekindle your passion for art, Japanese food, or dog shows, and it can satisfy your need for social contact outside of work and family. And just as with exercising, club meetings and classes force you to make time for your interests. Dedicating Monday nights to your Spanish lessons or Saturday mornings to drawing class helps keep them on your schedule.

Of course, we're not so foolish to think that you'll be able to maintain your prekids roster of activities. After all, you've got a new passion now—your little ones. But you can still keep up with your interests even when you can't pursue them with the vigor you once did. If finances or time prevent you from catching a concert that once upon a time would have been a must-see, at least play the CD in your car while you run errands. Hang a poster (from a favorite museum exhibit or of a sports hero you admire, for example) in your office or kitchen.

More easy ways to find an outlet for your passions:

- Read books and subscribe to magazines (even catalogs might do) that relate to your favorite hobbies.
- Go virtual: Sign up for E-mail listserves (scan a directory of them by visiting www.Liszt.com) and visit Internet chat rooms dedicated to your interests.
- Use your vacations—and even your business trips—to pursue your hobbies. You might schedule a trip to coincide with a quilters' convention or travel to New York if theater is your passion. Make room for a museum visit, a hike, or a shopping trip, if that's what you love, during whatever vacation you take.

WORKING MOM'S WORDS OF WISDOM

"Adapt Your Talents to Your Changing Life"

After my child reached age three, I was able to get back into hobbies that I hadn't been able to do for the past three years. My expectations have changed somewhat, too. Instead of painting as much as I used to, I paint and do art or science projects with my son for my much-needed artistic outlet.

—**Cinta Burgos,** *married, engineer, and mother of a four-year-old boy*

20

Being Part of Your Community

Okay, you might say. This is where I really must draw the line. There's just *no way* I have time to be involved in a charity, community, or volunteer organization. I have no time at all—so where would I find some to give away?

All true. Yet you might be surprised. There are plenty of good reasons to volunteer—some altruistic, some not so. And there truly are ways to find the time to do it. As with everything else in your life, it's a matter of prioritizing and organizing. If you decide to move volunteer work to a higher position on your ladder of priorities, you'll make room for it in your life.

Why Volunteer?

First, it makes you feel good. John Raynolds, a retired CEO, lifelong volunteer, and author of *The Halo Effect: How Volunteering Can Lead to a More*

Fulfilling Life—and a Better Career (now out in paperback under the title *Volunteering*) calls this "psychic income." Doing good for others gives you an incredible charge of pride, optimism, and energy. It can help add meaning to a life filled with a nonstop whirl of work-kids-eat-sleep. It adds purpose and another role to your life (see page 164 on the value of multiple roles).

Volunteering also sets a good example for your children. When they see you make a contribution to your community or your world, they're learning that one person can make a difference. They also see that not everyone is as lucky as they are and that we all need to pitch in to make our society function. Those are some pretty powerful lessons.

Your volunteer efforts can have a tangible, positive effect on your community—and "community" can mean your block, school district, city, state, country, or even the world. That benefits you, your children and family, your friends, your neighbors, and your coworkers.

Good works may even improve your health. Raynolds notes that many studies "have shown that volunteerism can result in a wide array of personal benefits, including greater longevity, increased self-acceptance, and reduced inner stress and conflict." If you're doing something you enjoy, a task that's meaningful, it becomes an activity you willingly make room for rather than a duty that must be squeezed into your tight schedule.

Volunteering—and this is John Raynolds's thesis—may even give your career a boost. Charity work and community involvement provide lots of opportunities for networking, whether you're looking for contacts, a new job, a role model or mentor, even a radical career change. Good works also provide an ideal venue for you to learn new skills and build your résumé.

Working mom Risa Greendlinger, the national manager of work/life initiatives for a child-care chain and the mother of four-year-old Shayna, has been volunteering since she was a teenager. Community service has become indelibly intertwined in her work and family life. "When it's all connected, the timing and the effort work out and everything fits," says Greendlinger. She's shared volunteer efforts with her mother and sister and found some of her jobs thanks to her community involvement efforts. Becoming a Big Sister to a little girl with HIV even helped her realize she was ready to be a mom!

Selecting an Activity

Of course, whatever you choose to devote your time to needs to be very fulfilling and meaningful for you. Think about what you enjoy and wish you could do more of. For example, if you're a city dweller you might wish you had more outdoor time; perhaps giving your time to a parks revitalization or community garden program would be right for you. If you're an art lover, you might choose to lead tours at a museum or teach arts and crafts classes to underprivileged kids (and hey, maybe your own kids could join in, too).

Or, think about what's missing in your life, advises John Raynolds. Is it social contact? Personal growth? Can you find a way to match this need with a volunteer organization that's eager for your help? If you've been meaning to add more spirituality to your life, for example, you might get involved with your synagogue's volunteer group or offer to teach Sunday school.

Consider practical matters, too. Would you prefer direct service, or do you feel you'll get more satisfaction from planning or fund-raising? Do you want to work in a group, or one-on-one with someone in need? Would you prefer to be indoors or out? Work in your own home making phone calls or designing a newsletter, or be hands-on at a hospital? Is there anything you want to avoid, such as the sight of blood or asking for money? Make these preferences a part of your decision-making process.

How to Find a Group That Needs Your Help

If you already know what cause makes you passionate, you're ready to go. But you may not know where to start. To seek out volunteer opportunities in your area, try:

- **Volunteer centers:** Most cities have one of these. It's a clearinghouse that helps match groups in need with volunteers looking for a cause to support. To find one in your area, check the phone book under "volunteers/voluntary" (in the white pages) or "social service" or "community organizations" (in the blue or yellow pages).

- **The United Way:** In addition to raising money, the United Way often refers volunteers to organizations needing support.
- **Your local library:** Ask for help at the reference desk. Your librarian can show you local, state, and national listings of community groups and advocacy organizations.
- **Religious organizations:** They often support an array of volunteer efforts.
- **Your child's school:** Schools are always looking for parent volunteers, whether via a parent-teacher association, a special parent involvement office, or one-shot efforts like a fund-raiser or field trip.
- **On the Internet:** Visit www.servenet.org, www.cns.gov (Corporation for National Service), and www.nonprofits.org (Internet Nonprofit Center) for ideas and information on organizations that need your help.
- **Books:** There are many books, such as John Raynolds's *Halo Effect,* that have detailed listings of volunteer-supported organizations.

Seven Ways to Make Time for Volunteer Work

1. Be choosy. Find an organization that's meaningful, works with your schedule, and values your time (see "How to Find a Group That Needs Your Help," page 169). "My main criteria is that they don't have a lot of planning meetings. Those are a waste of time," says one mom, an engineer and mother of one from Ohio. "If they can tell me what they need, I will go and get it done. Don't make me sit around for hours in the evening discussing what needs to be done. Just do it!"
2. See if your employer has a program allowing employees time off to volunteer. NationsBank, for example, gives its workers up to two hours *every week* to spend time working in their child's school,

and DaimlerChrysler Corporation gives its employees an hour a week to work in schools or give career advice to kids. A few rare companies, such as software maker Autodesk, even offer sabbaticals—large blocks of paid time off, which many employees use to pursue volunteer work. Mom Risa Greendlinger says that co-operation from her employer was the only way she kept up her volunteer commitments during a brief period when she and her husband lived apart after he took a new job in another city.

3. Select volunteer work that you can do with your husband and/or your children. There's no faster way to drive home the good lessons volunteerism can impart (see "Why Volunteer," page 167).
4. Enlist aid at crunch times. "When the girl I mentored as a Big Sister was hospitalized and my own daughter was small, I reached out for help," says Greendlinger. "At a Junior League meeting, I told fellow members that visiting Tamisha in the hospital every week was too much for me. A rotating group of members agreed to send little packages and write notes to Tamisha every day." Greendlinger says that she's always found that others are willing to support her: "People are eager to make a difference," she says.
5. Look for a volunteer job with a minimal commitment, at least at first. For example, instead of agreeing to teach reading every Tuesday evening, start by scheduling one Tuesday a month. You can always up your quotient later, if and when you find some more time to devote to your volunteer projects.
6. If you can't see your way clear to donating time, consider donating money instead. This can make you feel as if you've at least tried! Always check out the organization to which you plan to donate. You want to make sure that they are using most of their contributions for services, instead of for administration. Two resources: the National Charities Information Bureau (212-929-6300 or www.give.org) and the Philanthropic Advisory Service, which is part of the Better Business Bureau (703-276-0133 or www.bbb.org).
7. If all else fails, sit tight and wait. When you have very young children, it *is* very difficult to add volunteer work into the mix of

home, kids, and work (not to mention self). You may need to put your plans on hold for a while, as Risa Greendlinger did for a few months after she moved to rejoin her husband and took a new, challenging job. Consider keeping a notebook or file folder where you note ideas for organizations you'd like to get involved in when you have time. This will keep your toe in the water.

Epilogue
Working Moms' Time Is Now

This is the time for working mothers—almost 26 million women with children under the age of eighteen are in the labor force—and their positive influence on the way people work has had far-reaching effects. In 1982, 80 percent of all workers had nine-to-five jobs; today almost half of all employees can choose alternative schedules. The advent of the Family and Medical Leave Act and the increasing availability of on- or near-site child care are but two more examples of the positive pressure that working moms exert on government and corporate culture.

At home, too, working moms have created change—a *Working Mother* survey from 1979 led us to predict that working wives of tomorrow would balk at having to do the lion's share of running the house and taking care of the children and spouse. Today, according to sociologist Rosalind Barnett, men do 45 percent of total housework. Fifty years ago women controlled little of the nation's capital; today they own businesses, participate in the stock market, and have control of most high-end family expenditures.

But this good news doesn't mean that all working moms receive the fair and equal treatment they deserve or that our society has fully accepted the essential role it must play in helping to support the mothers' dual role as family member and employee. Too many women still worry about being penalized for attending to child-care emergencies; too many are intimidated by bosses who expect that work consistently be their top priority; too many single moms find themselves so weary from shouldering the pressures of work and family that they cannot attend to their own physical, emotional, or spiritual needs.

Working moms' time is now. And we should take advantage of the growing power we have. By working to increase sensitivity on the part of government and business to the vital needs of families and women, we will help working moms in the next century enjoy the times of their lives even more.

Index